# Copyright Law for Artists, Photographers and Designers

Gillian Davies

A & C Black · London

First published in Great Britain in 2010
A & C Black Publishers Limited
36 Soho Square
London W1D 3QY
www.acblack.com

ISBN 978-14081-24741

CIP Catalogue records for this book are available from
the British Library and the US Library of Congress.

Typeset in 10 on 13pt Celeste

Book design: Susan McIntyre
Cover design: Sutchinda Thompson
Commissioning Editor: Susan James

Printed and bound by Star Standard Pte Ltd, Singapore

This book is produced using paper that is made from
wood grown in managed, sustainable forests. It is
natural, renewable and recyclable. The logging and
manufacturing processes conform to the environmental
regulations of the country of origin.

# Contents

# Acknowledgements

I have tried to populate this book with anecdotal references from real living designers and artists, and where possible from lawyers and experts in this area. Unfortunately, there are few UK cases in which art copyright is contested, so few lawyers have had the opportunity to specialise in the area; moreover, many who do know a little are unwilling to share their knowledge for the common good. Thanks must therefore especially go to the following people who took the time to help me understand some difficult areas: Dids MacDonald (ACID Anti Copying in Design), Andrew Lee (McDaniel & Co. solicitors), Jonathan Lake QC (Axiom Advocates) and Ian C. Ballon (Greenberg Traurig, LLP).

Special thanks are due to the people who have shared their artworks with me to make this book the lovely thing I hope it is: Euan Myles, Thurle Wright, Kriket Broadhurst, Tami Cohen and Robin Frowley.

I am also grateful to and have been inspired by others who have worked in this area: Professor John Henry Merryman; Simon Stokes (for his clear-headed write-ups of the *Bridgeman* and *Molino* cases for the Institute of Art & Law); Ruth Cooper of the IAL; and US illustrator and copyright champion, Brad Holland.

I have two beautiful children. If it were not for my mum, Helen, I would never get any work done at all – art, law or otherwise. So, thank you, mum.

Gillian Davies
lawandarts@aol.com

# Preface

Copyright hopefully should never be a problem for any of us: in the normal run of business, visual creators are usually more concerned with trying to make a new work or earn a little cash or market their work online or to galleries, and keep ahead of basic things like income tax or VAT.

But the whole point of copyright law is that it is intended to **help artists**: it is an *economic right*: if you have spent time and effort creating something, copyright law is supposed to be there to ensure that if your work is re-used you will be a) *consulted* and b) paid. That's it in a nutshell. That and affording you protection, under moral rights, against 'derogatory treatments' of your art.

To quote a law book: Copinger and Skone James on Copyright 1980, as applied in a leading case about Arts & Crafts works, *Hensher*

*"Copyright law is ... the negative right of preventing the copying of physical material ... Its object is to protect the [artist] from the unlawful reproduction of his material".*

It is a 'negative right' – because it starts by saying the author/ originator has exclusive rights ('and therefore you do not ... so don't copy unless you ask and/or pay...') – but it is not a negative in the sense that as a legal tool it CAN be very strong and effective.

I am not sure enough has been made of this in recent times when people seem to be more worried that others are out there trying to use copyright to ringfence public domain work and to try to undermine sharing (cf Wikipedia/National Portrait Gallery debate, p.32–3).

Copyright can be a very positive, financial tool.

There are a number of reasons why I thought this little handbook for artists, photographers and designers would be useful.

1  There are no other easily accessible illustrated sources written in plain English that are not law books for lawyers, or American. And UK law is different.

5

2 Copyright is complicated. Most people think they know something about it but it is not what you think it is. And it is 'old': UK copyright was first promoted by Hogarth who campaigned for a law to protect his engravings and later lithographs. The UK copyright framework is now 300 years and very creaky – the legislation is like a tiny old lady trying to drive a Hummer: it all seems a bit ill-fitted at times, especially when it comes to digital copyright and the Internet. This problem has been highlighted for a long time for the gaming and music industries. But less so for situations affecting visual creators.

3 Hand in hand with a bit of basic contract law, copyright can help you as an artist and help artists as a community. But you also need to know how to fight back – what was that I read in a recent chain email, quoting Maya Angelou?: '... *you shouldn't go through life with a catcher's mitt on both hands; you need to be able to throw some things back*'. I am currently watching with interest a new battle being played out on Twitter: an individual Etsy artist tackling alleged copyright abuses by a large stationery retailer.

4 There is very little real black letter law on copyright for artists because very few cases make it to court. When they do make it to court or there is a dispute that gets in the papers but is settled out of court it is usually because people have fallen out with each other – and copyright is used as a weapon in the ensuing fight, cf *Antiquesportfolio,* a case where copyright issues sprang up off the back of a contractual ('I'm-not-paying-because-you-messed-up ... o-yes-you-are...') dispute.

Then there is the problem of access: access for artists to legal advice and access to information: I have been working as a law editor for 15 years and therefore have access to certain legal materials: but do you? UK law is currently reflected in the Copyright, Designs and Patents Act 1988: but if you go to the government website which publishes it, you see great big disclaimers saying this is actually not current law because it has not been updated. I have to use a paid-for subscription service to get the updated law. And lawyers are not good at sharing information for free. Also, art copyright specialists are pretty thin on the ground. And if you looked at the orphan works proposals in the Digital Economy Bill 2009–10, the changes (now abandoned; see p.79) – were hidden away on a clause entitled

'Designated authority for video games etc' which you wouldn't even have known had anything in the world to do with art.

Therefore, there are very few answers to our copyright problems and questions. BUT we should know the basic rules, and get an idea of the boundaries and opportunities. Armed with this book, you may even earn a bit of extra money – from work you have already created and is just sitting there, as it were, 'in the bank'. This is your starting point – signposting you to where to enquire further.

I have included email addresses or web addresses in picture captions – on purpose to identify the copyright owner – and wish everyone in the world would do the same to help on picture research/ rights clearance!

**Disclaimer**
I am an artist with a law degree who works with legal texts as a law editor and writer, I am not a lawyer and am not providing legal advice.

Gillian Davies, MA, LLB; lawandarts@aol.com; www.carouselmonkey.co.uk

# 1

# How Issues Can Crop Up: The basics

Law differentiates between 'real property' and 'intellectual property'. In other words, I can sell a painting but keep the copyright to it, or I can sell the copyright – for instance, so that someone can use the image on a poster – but keep the actual physical painting and sell that to someone else.

Likewise, I can buy the copyright (e.g., buy a licence to use the image in a photograph I want for this book). But I may not necessarily be sent the actual image I need (this happened!), because while one person may own the copyright, another person may have custody of the actual painting or a photograph of the painting. Indeed, several people may be involved, and often are, which is why the process of picture research and licensing can be so painful.

## Scenario I

I paint a painting. Joynte buys it from me because the colours go well with her newly decorated bedroom. The next year she repaints her room and burns my painting. She is perfectly entitled to do so. She bought it. She owns the real property. However, if she were to film the burning and then publish that film, or to half-burn it and display the half-burnt-out painting in public, she could be in breach of my copyright (see Chapter 10 and the Churchill portrait case).

## Scenario II

So forget the burning.

Before I sold the painting to Joynte I asked Paul to photograph it for me. When I sold Joynte the painting, she did not ask me to sell (she did not want me to 'assign' or 'license') the copyright to her; she just wanted the painting itself – this is the usual scenario because no one thinks about copyright until it becomes an issue later. So I retained copyright, and thus can use the digital photos Paul has taken for me on my website and in books and catalogues, etc. Or can I? Strictly speaking, when Paul took the photograph he created a new copyright. So I am the original 'creator' of the painting, but he too has copyright in the photos* – the photographic expression of the work. So if I use his photo and not one of my own, strictly speaking I should ask him to license or assign it to me. So in reality I can use my own photographs, but I can't use Paul's photos unless I get copyright permission from Paul.

## Scenario III

At the time of buying the painting Joynte also asked me for copyright – let us say, an *assignment* of copyright, which means I am granting her complete and full control of the copyright (see Chapter 17 and Leibovitz developments). She then publishes her photo of my painting in a magazine alongside her interior designs. She can do that (though, of course, if she is using a photographer she needs to take care over joint copyright ownership or even multiple copyright owners). The magazine will probably ask for copyright. In the event, the magazine that publishes the pictures overprints my painting with text obliterating most of the image or else distorts it so that it looks really bad. Can I complain? Perhaps I can. I may have assigned copyright but, unless I have specifically contracted otherwise, I do still have moral rights in spite of no longer having either the painting or the copyright. It depends what the magazine does with the image, but it could amount to 'derogatory treatment' (Op artist Bridget Riley once complained about a national newspaper which printed one of her works randomly in an article not about her or about art, but about the hallucinatory effect of drugs).

## Scenario IV

**Except for the moral right of false attribution which does not last so long (only 20 years after death; s.86 of the 1988 Act).

Joynte waits until the year 2111 and, by now a crabby old 101-year old, burns the painting. I died in 2040, so the work is no longer governed by copyright or moral rights (both of which** apply for the lifetime of the artist plus a further 70 years). She can film the destruction or do whatever she wants. (But note that the 'lifetime of the artist + 70 years' rule does not apply to works made before 1989; and some works which expired during the 1990s were renewed – for example, Beatrix Potter illustrations.)

## INFORMATION BANK

For the difference between 'assigning' and 'licensing' see Chapter 17.

# 2

# Not What You'd Think

I think one of the reasons I like copyright law is because it is so perverse: it seems to apply to things that we wouldn't necessarily expect it to apply to, in strange ways and with strange practical results.

The court cases are replete with oddness, too: 'Copyright law protects foxes better than hedgehogs,' said Lord Hoffman famously in the *Designers Guild* case (see Chapter 4).

Copyright applies in the protection of fine art, sculpture, jewellery, furniture, photography, architecture, textiles, graphics and sometimes fashion, but it also applies to 'weird' things like tickets; or a plastic mould for the heating plates of a sandwich-toaster (characterised as a 'sculpture' in *Breville Europe* v *Thorn EMI*); or a football pools coupon (*Ladbroke* v *William Hill*); or even to belt buckles.

However, it does not apply to ordinary objects that are 'commonplace'. For instance, in two textiles cases it could have been argued (but wasn't in either case) that the basic design was so ordinary and commonplace as to render complaints about a similar competing design irrelevant because there was no underlying copyright in the first place. One was the repeat classical pineapple motif of the fabric in *Nouveau Fabrics* v *Voyage Decoration and Dunelm Soft Furnishing*; the other involved the stripes and flowers of the *Designers Guild* case (see p.25).

But many artists depict ordinary objects. Can that mean they do not get copyright protection? Of course not. Tracey Kendall's feather and spoon screenprint banners; Norman Holland's *Cabbage (After Magritte)* 1995 colour photo (on BridgemanArt.com); my birds (see p.13); Kriket Broadhurst's ceramic jewellery (see p.14 and p.48) – it seems obvious to me that all of these would be copyright protected.

But what if a designer picks up on a general theme? I am thinking of Russian dolls as themes – themes of expensive brands like the wonderful Oilily from the Netherlands, which have been picked up by pretty much every retailer on the high street in recent years.

**Example: design and layout**

Magazine publisher IPC commenced legal proceedings in relation to their publication *Ideal Home* against the publishers Highbury for copyright infringement in its publication *Home*. It was argued that features of the design of *Ideal Home* as well as feature concepts had been unlawfully copied. According to a Design Council report, the claim failed on the grounds that the similarities found in Highbury's magazine originated from 'bog standard' design elements common to the industry, rather than unlawful copying of IPC's work.

It is not clear from the Design Council's summary whether a claim for passing off was considered; but perhaps it could have been (passing off is another form of intellectual property protection and is explained in Chapter 9).

## Nil creare?

...........................

*The Latin 'creare' alludes to the notion of creation from nothing.

As you will read in the chapters on Photography, you do not always need to be dealing in 'high art'/fine art. No massive amount of 'creativity' in the Latin sense of 'creare'* is needed for UK copyright to apply: on the contrary a work can still be copyrightable under UK law even if it is 'creation from something else': as long as it is original in the sense of not being copied, you are entitled to a new copyright (see Chapter 4).

Law students immediately learn that copyright is not there to protect ideas ('there is no copyright in an idea'), but to protect *expressions* of ideas. Of course this runs into difficulty when it comes to thinking about modern, conceptual artists. Take an artist like Roman Ondák, whose art in one instance consisted of photographing a queue of people; looking at the photo, you'd have to say the 'idea is the medium' – there is nothing intrinsically 'artistic' about it, no expression as such, just the idea. Or take Felix Gonzalez-Torres, who piled up a load of garbage (in this case tin cans) in the corner of a room. That could regarded as not copyright-protectable just because it is commonplace.

Of course, those artists were flouting all notions of traditional art and classification anyway, so the assumption is that they would not have cared if theoretically they might not be meet the requirements of copyright protection under current UK law. But the art world would certainly not be ruling them out as artists just because they were 'ideas men'.

Gillian Davies, *Quartet* (detail). Mixed media collage, 2008. I paint a lot of birds. Birds are 'commonplace', so can someone just copy this picture exactly or reproduce it without my permission? I think not, though if it got to court it might be arguable.
© Gillian Davies, lawandarts@aol.com/ Paul Ditch Fixed Focus. Photography: fixed.focus@ymail.com

## It doesn't even need to be 'real'

Copyright protection is also afforded to computer-generated works and to software. Gaming-industry designers will find a US development of interest here.

Well-known 'massively multiplayer online game' *Second Life* allows users to assume virtual personalities and to create their own virtual worlds. Eight million residents live within the game, even being able to trade and make money (paid in fictitious Linden

Kriket Broadhurst, sterling silver hand-beaten ring with hand-crafted ceramic bead, 2009. Bead, made by the artist, 1.5cm (½ in.) long. kriketdesigns@gmail.com. Kriket makes jewellery to showcase her hand-crafted beads, which have a glossy, opulent effect. Based on the 5000-year-old Ancient Egyptian faience technique, the beads are self-glazing due to the oxides and base materials in Kriket's recipes. But would another jeweller using the same faience technique with similar colours and materials be in breach of her copyright?

dollars, which can be converted into real cash dollars). A sought-after trophy in the game was the SexGen bed, which sold for $45 and allowed the player-avatars to have virtual sex. A resident named Stroker Serpentine (real name Kevin Alderman, owner of virtual *Second Life* company Eros) designed and sold the bed within *Second Life*. In 2007 a legal action citing US copyright law and trade marks law was instigated under party names *Eros* v *John Doe* against Linden Labs, and also against PayPal, AT&T and Charter Communications, requesting them to block sales by another *Second Life* resident who started selling a lookalike bed for $15. It was claimed that the lookalike bed was visually identical but in addition had been created by circumventing technology protections in order to repeat the code and graphics of the virtual bed – which would be a clear violation of the US Digital Millennium Copyright Act 2000 (s.1201). Linden Labs wanted the issues dealt with under its self-regulatory, in-world 'abuse reporting' system. At the time of going to press the case was still ongoing in the US District Court for Northern California.

You might protest that copyright law is intended to protect real-life intellectual property and so this virtual world discussion seems odd, but in fact there was evidence of the copying of software, so potentially it was 'real' copyright theft. If the case had arisen under UK law it would probably have been heard under computer-software copyright.

## What if someone copies my style?

We've established that there is no copyright in ideas, but what if the artwork is more or less defined by its style, by the way in which it is created? And what if someone copies pretty much identically a technique which gives the artwork its whole essence, its signature?

Thurle Wright is an established London-based artist (below and p.17). She works with paper, old books and pamphlets, creating large-scale, very beautiful and intricate 3D sculptural works that are sometimes wall-mounted and sometimes freestanding or hung from the ceiling. There are several other artists who have exhibited in London galleries who work with the same materials in a similar way, and it is possible for suspicions to arise, whether founded or not. 'How much is subconscious?' asks Thurle. 'How much do we take from others without realising?' This is difficult territory, and causes concern to many artists.

Thurle Wright, *Dictionary Obsession*, 2009. Pages from a pocket dictionary, blue ink on paper 30 x 30cm (12 x 12in.). © Thurle Wright. thurle@hotmail.com

Another situation might be where an advertising agency commissions a graphic artist to produce, say, a book cover. The design is rejected, a 'kill fee' paid, and nothing more said about it. But later the agency asks another artist to attempt the same commission and shows the original rejected artwork, asking the second artist to do it 'a bit like that but make a few tweaks'. The second artwork seems to have the same 'flavour' as the first: same idea, same colours, same scale, similar style. Is B an infringing copy of A? The agency should not have commissioned the work in that way, but the reality is that this sort of thing happens all the time.

The bottom line is that it is hard to ring-fence this kind of thing but you should nevertheless seek legal advice if you are worried that someone has 'stolen' your concept. Things like this can often be fended off by a lawyer's letter.

**Remember:** if your work came first chronologically, and you can prove that; if the other work seems to be copying a 'substantial part' of your work in terms of quality not quantity; and if the other work appears to be copying yours – i.e. it is not original and the other artist is becoming economically enriched at your expense – you may well have a good case under copyright law to have the other work taken out of circulation.

In addition to copyright law, there is a small possibility that you could use the law of passing off (see Chapter 9). Alternatively, you could invoke 'constructive trust' to help protect yourself from cheeky copying, the idea being that if you tell/show someone something in confidence, they become a trustee of that information and thus owe you a duty of care.

So if Thurle sent images of her work to a gallery and heads her communications 'in confidence' and 'copyright Thurle Wright 2010', then if the gallery later uses her image on its website without asking her, they could be in breach of trust as well as breach of copyright. Another thing she could do on a practical level is to send a copy of the letter and artwork to a lawyer or to ACID (see Resources p.94) saying 'This letter and the attached image [specify details] was copied to ACID's databank/solicitors [specify name] on [date]...'.

Thurle Wright, *Dodecahedron Dreaming* (maquette), 2007. Paper, card, glue, found figure. 51 cm (20in.) diameter. Text taken from six books: *The Travels of Marco Polo, Don Quixote, Tales from the Arabian Nights, The Lost World, The Iliad, Around the World in 80 Days.*
© Thurle Wright.
thurle@hotmail.com

## INFORMATION BANK

*Breville Europe* v *Thorn EMI* (1985) [1995] FSR 77; and see *Arnold* v *Miaferen* [1980] RPC 397.

*Ladbroke (Football) Ltd* v *William Hill (Football) Ltd* [1964] 1 WLR 20.

Pineapple case: *Nouveau Fabrics* v *Voyage Decoration and Dunelm Soft Furnishings.* [2004] EWHC 895 (Chancery).

*Second Life* case: *Eros, Llc et al* v *Linden Research, Inc et al*, US District Ct, California Northern (Oakland); Case 4:09cv4269.

Norman Holland's *Cabbage (After Magritte)*, 1995, colour photo (on BridgemanArt.com – image NDS 236979).

*PC Media* v *Highbury Leisure Publishing* (2004) http://www.designcouncil.org.uk/en/About-Design/Business-Essentials/Intellectual-property/Ten-examples

www.thurle.com

# 3

# Commissioning

Under present UK copyright law, the person who commissions an artwork does not keep the copyright in it; the copyright is vested with the creator. That is the default position.

## Scenario I

So I, a fine artist, commission a graphic design for my art business from US logo whizz Tami Cohen. The copyright in the logo is Tami's, not mine (s.11 of the 1988 Copyright Act) – that is, unless I ask her either to assign the copyright to me (in which case I get all copyright rights) or to *license* it to me (in which case I get certain agreed rights). Licensing is what usually happens, and if you are dealing commercially with graphic or web designers, for example, it is best to contract upfront all envisaged uses including copyright and any other intellectual property (IP) permissions.

As it happens I didn't pay Tami any cash; I gave her one of my screenprints as a quid pro quo. But this doesn't necessarily have any bearing on the situation because it doesn't matter if I have paid her cash or cash equivalent for copyright (though this does matter for design rights). However, if Tami had been my employee, the copyright would have been mine.

## Scenario II

I am commissioned by Matthew to paint his portrait. He loves it so much he wants to keep it for himself, gazing at it daily like Dorian Gray, and not publish it in any way. I'm proud of my painting and spent many years of my life in love with Matthew, so I put it up on Facebook, Twitter, Flickr, my blog and on websites of various free art image banks as part of my art portfolio. Matthew is in a rage but cannot stop me (but with a small caveat in relation to privacy rights – see Chapter 6). He should have got me to assign copyright upfront.

That is the default position. But you can also contract to cancel this out or change it. And in certain scenarios, perhaps where there

# Carousel Monkey

is a clear commercial flavour to the situation, the default position can be reversed: a court may decide that the commissioner *does* keep or get copyright in the work commissioned, as happened in the *Durand* v *Molino* case (see below).

However, if the portrait had been painted before 1st August 1989, the opposite would be true. Matthew, as its commissioner, would be the copyright owner (see the Winston Churchill example in Chapter 10).

To summarise, if you commission artwork, copyright is not the commissioner's but the creator's, unless, that is, she licenses or assigns copyright or unless there are very unusual circumstances. But for older works of art, commissioned before the 1988 Act came into force, the reverse is true. The commissioner did indeed get copyright under the old law. And for design rights, the commissioner of an unregistered design is the first owner of copyright under the 1988 Act (s.215) (see Chapter 9).

## The twist in the tale

The legal authority for the twist in the tale is the case of *Durand* v *Molino*, involving a painter to the UK Royal Family, Andrew Durand.

Mario Molino ran a pizza restaurant called Da Mario. He commissioned three paintings: one entitled *Four Seasons*; one, *Pizza*

19

*Diana 1996* depicting himself handing Princess Diana a pizza (in 1996); and a third work, *Princess Diana 1997*, which was a repainted version of the second. The court case involved copyright claims surrounding all three paintings. Mario paid partly in cash and partly in kind for the artworks and for licences to use the images on various bits of stationery and merchandising.

Durand claimed that Molino exceeded his rights and went beyond the scope of his licence by getting different bits of stationery and merchandising made up, purportedly under the original licences (and getting away without paying further sums for these commercial uses).

## Four Seasons

This painting, 'a portrait of Molino with members of his family and friends', was commissioned by Molino for the restaurant's walls, and there was also agreement that the image could be used reprographically as a menu cover. Durand objected to the further use of the image on matchbooks, greetings cards, postcards and business cards. He also asserted that the picture was intended to be hung in a restaurant in Spain that Molino also owned.

Molino's lawyers conceded that Durand was the legal owner of the copyright but claimed that (i) they were beneficially entitled to use the painting as they did, and that (ii) the *Four Seasons* contract provided that Durand would assign the copyright to Molino on demand, or that the defendants had at least an implied licence to use the work for the commercial purposes of Da Mario.

The court favoured Molino's position. It held that Molino was 'beneficially entitled' to use the painting in the ways he had done. This is an odd piece of law – not commercial/copyright law but a piece of equity law (and, by the way, there is no equity in Scotland, so we don't know what would happen if the situation arose there).

The court also agreed with Molino's solicitors in saying that in any case, Molino had an implied exclusive licence to use the painting for the commercial purposes he had devised. Moreover, the court decreed that if Durand had felt abused in any way and had wished to exercise his rights, he is protected under moral rights, implying that he should perhaps have pursued the case on the basis of a moral rights claim (see Chapter 10). One of the main points about the painting was that it was commissioned specifically for a commercial use – to show the restaurateur in his restaurant and specifically to be hung in that restaurant. This influenced the court in its decision in favour of the commissioner.

Here is an extract from the ruling (High Court of Justice (Chancery Division) 10 July 1999):

> With regard to *Four Seasons*
> (1) The reason why Molino commissioned the *Four Seasons* was clearly commercial, as a means of depicting Molino and his associates in the context of Da Mario as a business venture. This being a portrait which was commissioned in a commercial context with a view to its exhibition in Da Mario and its reproduction on items such as menus, Molino must at least be entitled (i) to prevent the copying of his portrait by others and (ii) to enjoy a perpetual exclusive licence to use the copyright-protected work. Prima facie, Molino, being both the party commissioning the portrait and its subject, should have full control of the work.
> (2) Durand, as author, was the first owner of copyright in *Four Seasons*. However, Molino was beneficially entitled to the copyright, which had to be transferred to him (*Ray* v *Classic FM plc* [1998] FSR 622 applied).
> (3) Despite Molino's legal entitlement with regard to *Four Seasons*, Durand was protected in relation to any adverse forms of exploitation of the painting by Molino, by the moral rights provisions in the Copyright, Designs and Patents Act 1988 that prohibited derogatory treatment of the work and that entitled him to be identified as the author when reproductions were issued to the public.

*Pizza Diana 1996*   Durand retained copyright, but allowed/licensed Molino to use the image on menus, invitations and greetings cards. Durand complained that by getting postcards and greetings cards made up with textual overprinting, he was in breach of copyright.

Again the court favoured Molino's position. It simply held that overprinting 'did not change a licensed work into an unlicensed work', and that there had therefore been no breach of copyright. (Again it would seem that a moral rights argument might have held more sway.)

The case is also interesting because it raised legal issues concerning the rights of freelance photographers and the responsibilities/liabilities of artwork owners. Molino had hosted an open evening at which a freelance press photographer was present. The photographer took pictures of the painting, which were subsequently printed in the national press (various papers).

The copyright point here relates to Molino's potential responsibility (liability) to Durand for permitting the photographer to take pictures of the work, as under the 1988 Copyright Act you can be indirectly as well as directly liable for copyright infringements (see third-party liability, p.88). Here Molino could have been considered to be 'authorising' the infringement of Durand's copyright by the photographer (and subsequently by the newspapers). However, the court was quite robust and firm in standing by Molino again, saying (to paraphrase), 'no, there is clear case law to say that to authorise infringement you need to do *something more* than a negative ... simply standing around and allowing photography to happen does not make you culpable'.

This is good news for art galleries and museums in charge of wilful visitors with cameras, though it has to be said that the *Molino* case does not absolve galleries, museums and others from taking responsibility for putting people on notice of the fact that photography is likely NOT to be permitted (see Chapter 16).

## What does it all mean?

In short, the *Molino* case means that, in the logo situation above, if I want to prevent others from using my logo, or I want to register a trade mark, even though I have not contracted with Tami to get the copyright, legally I might still be regarded as having 'beneficial ownership' of the logo, despite the default position that the copyright belongs to Tami, not me. So I could still enjoy certain rights as well as Tami having them. I could also argue that I have an implied licence for certain usages.

## R Griggs Group (2003)

Another more recent case involving a logo seems to agree with *Molino* (i.e. it seems to make exceptions to the rule that the commissioner does not get copyright). Griggs, the maker of Dr Martens boots, indirectly commissioned a designer to produce a new logo. IP ownership was not satisfactorily dealt with by contract. A dispute arose over the amount the job was worth, and the designer also claimed that he still owned copyright in what he had created. The court disagreed, holding that in the circumstances Griggs should be considered beneficial owner of the copyright.

## What does it really mean?

Under present UK copyright law, the person who commissions an artwork does not keep the copyright in it – the copyright is vested in the creator. That is the default position. But, if you found yourself in a situation where you wanted lawyers to argue to the contrary, there is plenty of leeway in the law. So, to avoid any messiness it is simply safer and better to sort it all out contractually under licence or assignment in advance.

## Red alert: older works of art

Everything written above is wrong in relation to works made before 1st August 1989: the predecessor statute of 1956 said the exact opposite, namely that '... where a person commissions the taking of a photograph, or the painting or drawing of a portrait, or the making of an engraving, and pays or agrees to pay for it in money or money's worth, and the work is made in pursuance of that commission, the person who so commissioned the work shall be entitled to any copyright subsisting therein...'. (s.4(3), 1956). This applies to all such works unless there is an agreement to the contrary.

And the first owner of copyright in photographs taken before 1st August 1989 is – and this sounds quite archaic now – the person who owned the material on which the image was made (say, a newspaper in the case of freelance photographers given film by their commissioning editors).

## INFORMATION BANK

Design rights and commissioning: http://acid.eu.com/ip-doctor-faq

Dr Martens: http://www.designcouncil.org.uk/en/About-Design/Business-Essentials/Intellectual-property/Ten-examples.

'Matthew': NB if Matthew had commissioned the portrait as a photograph or a film (not a painting) for 'private and domestic' purposes he could stop me from publishing the image (s.85 1988 Act).

# 4

# Too Close for Comfort: Quality not quantity

You may have copied someone else's work to some extent, or 'tributed' or 'adapted' it, but did you copy a 'substantial part' so that another artist would be entitled to start a copyright action?

There is an immense amount of room for legal argument on this subject, so if you are yourself copying an artist's work, you have to be able to explain why your work is a new and original work, and thus entitled to a separate copyright, and not a copy of another work.

Likewise, if you find someone else copying your work, there are ways in which it would be possible to argue that it is copyright-infringing: if you can convince the courts that your work came first in time; and that a 'substantial part' (s.16(3), 1988 Act) of your work – or even the entire work – has been taken by the new work. The bottom line is copyright law seeks to prevent one person appropriating the 'skill and labour' of another. But there are a lot of grey areas here, as the following discussion of the leading case, which concerned printed fabric designs, reveals.

## The *Designers Guild* case

In the year 2000 the House of Lords developed the legal test that still applies to determine whether there has been an illegal/infringing copy. In *Designers Guild* v *Russell Williams*, five Law Lords were asked to look at a previous decision of the Court of Appeal. In so doing they delivered five leading judgments which represent current law on copyright. Unfortunately for us, those five judgments are not necessarily concurring. Indeed, they are not always complementary, and at one point there is, in my view, flat contradiction, or at least circularity.*

---

*The author is influenced in this by the analysis of the barrister for Designers Guild, Jonathan Turner, who has written, 'There were differences in analysis in the respective speeches, which may reflect an unarticulated conceptual difference as to whether the copyright work is the subject-matter itself (painting, text, music etc.) or the creative work and skill which is expended to produce it.' www.jonathanturner.com/Copyright.htm 'When Is Inspiration Unlawful?'

*Ixia* fabric, Designers Guild from the law report at [1998] FSR 803 (by kind permission of Sweet & Maxwell).

*Marguerite* fabric, Washington DC (Russell Williams (Textiles) Ltd), from the law report at [1998] FSR 803 (by kind permission of Sweet & Maxwell). In trying to defend its case, Washington DC, the trading name for Russell Williams (Textiles) Ltd, presented 30 different colourways to the court. According to Washington DC, the FSR report publishes the colourway that looks closest to the Designers Guild textile – cream and terracotta (as here).

The judgment needs to be treated with care and allows for various different arguments to be run under it, but in essence it says the following:

(1) Copyright law is different from the law of passing off (see Chapter 9). If it were passing off, you could ask, 'Did the creator of B copy A such that she would dupe onlookers into thinking B is A'? But that is not the question to ask in assessing breaches of copyright (says the House of Lords).

(2) Invoking copyright law, if you look at the predecessor work, A (the thing that came first), and compare it with the second work, B (the thing that is alleged to be breaching the copyright of A), you need to look at the works as a whole, and to see if there are similarities, and you then need to decide if work B has copied a substantial part of work A.

(3) 'Substantial part' is a *qualitative* assessment, not a *quantitative* one. There is no need to show that a large percentage of the original design has been copied, but rather that an important part, or parts, of the original design has been taken. The question of whether a 'substantial part' has been copied, said the House of Lords, should be answered by considering only the original design – at this stage, there is no longer any reason to consider the copy design and compare it with the original. So anything you may have heard about being able to copy a certain percentage or a certain number of elements from an image, you can forget. It's about quality, about which the court – not you and not the 'experts' – will be the ultimate arbiter.

**Myth:** A jeweller/designer I spoke to told me a she was taught at college that 'as long as something is changed by more than 10 per cent then it can be copied'. That is wrong. It is about quality not quantity. But what does that mean? The law is very grey here.

Lord Millett also set up what in this author's view is a very odd test: he said that, because this is not the law of passing off, you are not permitted to use simply your own subjective judgment to decide if B breaches A's copyright. Instead you have to apply a technical legal test, as follows:

1 Identify the parts of work B which A says are infringing, looking not at the whole work but at specifics. At this stage the court might decide to discount things that are commonplace (e.g.

here the court might see that, specifically, flowers and stripes are present in both designs, but then effectively say, 'So what? Everyone is entitled to draw flowers and stripes so there can't be any copyright case.').

2  If A can show there are enough specific similarities, then B has to convince the court why B's work is *not* an infringing copy (the 'onus of proof' switches to B).

3  if the court favours A's argument, then it needs to decide if B has taken a 'substantial part' of A's work. This depends on the importance of that part to work A, so you look at work A when considering 'substantial part', not work B.

So take my seagull pictures (drawn on a little handheld Nokia N800 for the *I Can Draw* project; p.28). I 'copied' the seagull from a photograph in a child's book on nature. I did copy it – I am admitting I copied it. Under Lord Millett's 'substantial part' argument just outlined, my seagull picture could well be an infringing copy of the photo under UK copyright law – if you look at the photo, a significant and substantial part of that image is the pose/motif of the subject. However, the two final images do not look markedly the same: the original is a colour photograph, predominantly grey, of a seagull in flight in this position; the character of the computer drawings is entirely different. I just copied the rough shape of the bird in flight (see *Bauman* v *Fussel*, below, which I feel must be similar on the facts). To reprise Lord Millett's ruling: '... while the copied features must be a substantial part of the copyright work [work A], they need not form a substantial part of the defendant's work [work B] ... the overall appearance of [work B] may be very different from the copyright work, but it does not follow that [work B] does not infringe [ A's] copyright.'

So even if you have made substantial changes you can still be in breach of copyright. So my computer doodles could be in breach of the photograph's copyright (I did want to reproduce the original photograph here, but the publisher did not respond to my enquiry).

On the other hand, it might not be infringing. As another Law Lord, Lord Scott, said, even if you sit with work A at your hand, you can still create a new copyright: 'Even where there is direct evidence of copying, *as, e.g., where it is admitted that the copier has produced his "copy" with the original at his elbow*, the differences ... may be so extensive as to bar a finding of infringement. It is not a breach of copyright to borrow an idea ... and translate that idea into a new work.'

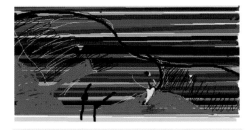

Gillian Davies, *Seagull I*, computer drawing using Nokia N800 for the *I Can Draw* project, Newcastle 2009. © Gillian Davies 2009.

Gillian Davies, *Seagull II*, computer drawing using Nokia N800 for the *I Can Draw* project, Newcastle 2009. © Gillian Davies 2009.

In essence what this seems to mean is that you can still be infringing copyright even if your work makes significant changes to a work it refers to. But equally, you can still be creating a separate, new copyright work, even if you have copied some part of another person's work.

It is interesting to note that in *Designers Guild*, witnesses for the defenders (Russell Williams) were not trusted in court: 'similar fact' evidence was presented by the lawyers to show they had done this sort of thing before (Osborne & Little had made a similar prior complaint against Russell Williams). The court seemed to be influenced by this.

**Note:** *This author believes that the* Designers Guild *case makes it potentially easier for a pursuer to take an action against an infringing copier: it is now open to argument that image B copies image A substantially, looking at things qualitatively rather than quantitatively. Very complex arguments could be advanced on both sides, in fact, so the decision in some ways is not that helpful.*

**Postscript:** This case was formidably punitive on the company that lost it. Designers Guild was awarded £10,000 in damages, but a spokesperson for Washington DC told me that it cost their business around £980,000 overall. This is, perhaps, an object lesson in getting insured (see Chapter 18, Getting Legal Advice), and there is no doubt the trial was emotionally draining for those involved with it – it lasted for five years, after all. 'These things ruin lives,' said the spokesperson:

We had evidence that our design was conceived using original reference materials, but we didn't have an expert witness; they [Designers Guild] did. And there were other unfairnesses about the trial, including loss of evidence. If a designer cannot put together a flower with some stripes and show how she came about the design, I don't know where designers can go ... This is a nightmare judgment. I am still mystified about why we were told that we could continue to print flowers only (on muslin) but banned from putting together stripes and flowers. I feel as if merely making an accusation of copying seals the deal [The onus of proof is on the accused to prove innocence – see onus of proof, above], i.e. the courts will agree that it is indeed copying. The power imbalance between smaller companies and larger companies is very noticeable.

(Designers Guild was invited to comment but did not.)

Sadly this is the current, quite confusing state of copyright law. The earlier case of *Bauman* v *Fussel* (which is not current law but which seems to this author to have represented a more commonsense approach) is summarised here for historic interest.

## Painting from photo: *Bauman* v *Fussell* (1953)

This case involved a painting of a cockfight, sold by an art dealer to a private individual, and a photographer whose colour photograph of a cockfight in Cuba was published in *Picture Post* magazine. The photographer accused the painter of infringing his copyright by reproducing it, demanded the painting be returned by the owner, and sought damages from the dealer. He lost in the trial and on appeal. The courts granted a new copyright to the painter because the painting was sufficiently different *not* to be a substantial copy. The photographer contended that the design and relative positions of the birds – the motif, as it were – represented a 'substantial part' of the image and therefore it was unlawful copying. The painter contended that this design/set-up was accidental – to be found in nature – and that therefore the photographer could not claim copyright in the relative positions of the birds which he just happened upon and did not create. In addition, the quality and feel of the two images was different: the photograph depended very heavily for its effects on the birds' relative positions but also on heightened shadow and lighting; the painting on the other hand did not use such lighting effects but instead was 'red' and 'bloody' evoking 'fury'. The court found that the painter had added a 'vigour' and 'life' to the birds which was lacking in the photograph.

It would be very interesting to see what would happen now if the same two images went before the Court of Appeal, which would now have to apply the *Designers Guild* 'substantial part' test. It might well be that the photographer would have a better chance of success post-*Designers Guild*.

## INFORMATION BANK

*Designers Guild Ltd* v *Russell Williams (Textiles) Ltd (t/a Washington DC)* 2000 WL 1720247, House of Lords [2000] 1 WLR 2416; [2001] 1 All ER 700. (Designers Guild was supported by ACID: see Chapter 18).

*Bauman* v *Fussell* [1978] RPC 485.

*I Can Draw* project: for further details contact Derrick Welsh: derrick.welsh@gmail.com

# 5

# Photography I

Photographs are perhaps the hardest artworks to deal with in terms of copyright law. To put it another way, UK copyright law was 'invented' before photography (1735 saw the first statute for works in the visual arts, created to deal with engravings and later lithography) and so has had to adapt – not necessarily very happily – to meet situations involving photographs, in the same way as copyright law is being bent very tortuously to try to deal with the internet.

Current UK copyright law is contained in a 1988 statute, as applied by case law.

**Myth**: Photos are 'not creative enough' to warrant copyright protection. That is wrong. There is no question that photographs are covered by copyright law. Indeed, things may be said to have reached the quite bizarre stage that any photograph will be protected by copyright, regardless of artistic merit, as long as it is original. You have to assume that all photographs are protected by copyright. There are a few exceptions, but it is safest to assume all photographs are protected – from Andy Goldsworthy and the output of professional fine art and advertising photographers, to the output of journalist photographers and private, non-skilled individuals.

Under current UK copyright law, you need only a very low standard of creative input for copyright to arise. So if there has been any investment in time and an element of originality, copyright can arise in a visual work. It doesn't need to be 'good' in the eyes of a court of law or indeed in the eyes of you or me.

Only if a photograph has been taken using no skill and effort whatsoever, perhaps using some form of mechanical means – such as a photocopier machine or enlargement facility or Computer

Numerical Control (CNC) machine – will it not be protected by copyright in itself as distinct from the object of which it is a photograph.

**How come?**

The leading case is *Bridgeman* v *Corel*. Corel produced a CD-rom of Old Master paintings (*Professional Photos CD Rom Masters*, including *The Laughing Cavalier* painted by Frans Hals in 1624), buying them from a company called Off the Wall Images. Bridgeman Art Library claimed that 120 of those images were in breach of its copyright, because although the paintings themselves were out of copyright (and in the 'public domain'), Bridgeman had not authorised anyone else to use its photographs (transparencies and digital image files) of the paintings and therefore Corel's use must have been in breach of Bridgeman's copyright.

The US court that decided the case, however, said that the Bridgeman Art Library's digital photographs of Old Master paintings were not sufficiently original to obtain copyright protection, and that therefore the software maker Corel had not breached copyright by using the images on a CD-rom.

That decision has since been questioned by UK legal experts who believe that, on the contrary, Bridgeman's photographic images did have copyright, and should have been protected, and that Corel should have had to pay, or at least get permission for use of Bridgeman's images.

So, if you go with the US court, an art library or museum or website provider setting up an online gallery using photographs which are simply 'mechanical' or 'slavish' copies of artworks would not necessarily have copyright in those slavish-copy photographs, meaning that potentially someone else could use them. But applying the same example to a case in the UK, Wikipedia's use of the National Portrait Gallery's images, the NPG would have copyright, and Wikipedia (or the individual 'John Doe', Derek Coetzee, now represented by the Electronic Frontier Federation [EFF] had better get the lawyers in. By the time this book is published that case may have been settled or decided, and in the process may have created an important new legal precedent.

This alternate view of UK copyright law says that it has always been accepted that a photographer – even if taking an image of a still object such as another person's artwork – still needs skill in arranging and lighting and focusing, etc., and therefore is entitled to copyright in the photograph – which is separate and distinct from the copyright in the picture itself. As an artist myself, I would be happy to go along with this, as it seems to make sense: I can paint (sometimes) but I can't take good-quality high-resolution images of my work such as would be good enough to put on the front cover of a glossy magazine. I use another skilled person, the photographer Paul Ditch, to do this for me. I have copyright in my artwork; Paul has copyright in the photograph of my artwork – unless or until I ask him (or a magazine or someone else asks him) to assign it to me (or them).

Wikipedia/National Portrait Gallery needs to go to court as a test case here, as we clearly cannot manage for long not knowing which is right.

## Open for argument: what is a 'slavish copy'?

What is also not crystal clear is what exactly fits into this doubtful category of 'slavish copy'. The US court in the *Bridgeman* case established that 'slavish copies' might not have the benefit of copyright protection. But what does that mean in practice? One judge suggested that it covers 'a photograph of a photograph or other printed matter'. But in *Bridgeman* we are talking about photographs of Old Master paintings. So where is the line drawn?

There is another case we should take note of because it could be a bit more helpful. In *Antiquesportfolio* the High Court decided that copyright existed in photographs taken of antiques (the photos here were used on a website by an antiques dealer's web designer, transformed into icons – navigation buttons and a banner – on the website).

The antiques store commissioned designers Rodney Fitch and Co. to provide the website and business stationery. Fitch used images taken from *Miller's Antiques Encyclopedia* for part of the website design – photographs of glassware, furniture, metalwork, etc.

The designer's argument (or his lawyers' argument) in that case was that the photos used as web icons within a website banner and as navigation buttons were photos of static objects and therefore did not have copyright in the first place. The argument did not win; the photos of the antiques did have copyright, said the court, which belonged to the publisher of the book, Reed Consumer Books 1998. The court was persuaded that the original photographs in the book had been taken with enough skill (positioning of an object, chosen angle, lighting, focus, choice of item and arrangement) to merit copyright protection, even though they are somewhat mundane shots of static 3D objects.

The court further said that the transformation of the photographs into web icons was a copyright-infringing use because, '[the photographs] appear to have been lifted straight from the *Encyclopedia*, albeit after photocopying, reduction in size and translation onto the screen'.

However, the logos – another element of the website design – the court deemed to have been 'transformed', as not enough of the original quality of the photographs remained in the logos on the website, and therefore they could not be regarded as infringing copies. The logos apparently consisted of traced outlines of the photographed objects, e.g. a traced outline of a candelabra.

The important part of the case for me is that because the photographs used by the web designer were protected by copyright, his having used them amounted to a breach of his contract with the antiques store – specifically, a breach of an implied term as to the use of reasonable skill and care in undertaking the work, meaning that he should have supplied images which had been copyright-cleared (licensed) or were free of copyright because in the public domain and 'out of copyright' (see Chapter 14).

Luckily for the designer the court did not go so far as to agree with Antiquesportfolio.com to the extent of allowing them to repudiate the contract (i.e. not pay monies due). But, given the difficulties, there had to be further court battles to decide upon the amounts owed to the various parties.

The lesson to learn is that if you use photographs for anything, you need to get copyright permission from someone for their use, unless, that is, you are clearly the only copyright owner or the photograph is clearly out of copyright. That is not easy to determine so it is best always to assume you need permission. New legal developments in relation to 'orphan works' were supposed to make this kind of situation clearer. But the proposals have been (temporarily?) abandoned (see Information Bank on p.79).

## Grey area

It seemed to matter to the trial judges in *Antiquesportfolio* that the icons used the whole of the photographic image, albeit reproduced small. But what if they'd just used a part? A lot was said about correct siting and lighting to reveal glazes, veneers, etc. on the furniture, but what if the items were 2D in this web graphics scenario?

It is clear that you should always expect that a photograph will have its own copyright separate from the thing it is a photograph of, and that photographers create copyright just as readily as illustrators or craftspeople or painters or sculptors, no matter how 'good' or 'bad' any of the creators or the images produced appear to be. That is, unless you're prepared to argue to the contrary, citing the *Bridgeman* case. Good luck!

# 6

# Photography II

We have already established that the person who commissions an artwork does not have copyright in it – the copyright is the creator's. That is the default position. But this is worth considering in the context of photography.

## Professional photography, freelancers and publication

Professional advertising photographer Euan Myles supplied an image of a thistle to a graphic design company for an album cover. Some time later the graphic design company contacted the photographer to complain that someone had used a very close version of the image in another context, without the graphic design company's permission. The photographer told the design company that he had not licensed or assigned copyright to them and therefore it was not really their 'cause' to argue, as the graphic design company was wrong in thinking the second image was in breach of 'their' copyright. The photographer is correct in asserting his rights.

## Case study: performance/ magazine photos

In another (hypothetical) scenario, Will Gompertz, a director of the Tate Gallery, performs in an experimental show on the Edinburgh Fringe. *Double Art History* is a fast-moving romp through the history of modern art; it is serious in that it covers a lot of excellent ground revising the history of modern art, but it is also typical audience-involving, self-parodying Fringe entertainment. Gompertz has a freelance photographer take stills of his performance and his audience because he wants to publish these exclusively in a Tate publication (though he might also want to use them in an article he is writing for the *Guardian*).

However, the freelance photographer, Jack Bailey, has the right to sell the pictures he takes for Gompertz to a photo agency or magazine unless Gompertz can be said to be employing the photographer – unlikely if he is freelance – or unless Gompertz gets Bailey to assign or license copyright to him. Alternatively, Gompertz could choose to fight the photographer in court, citing the *Molino* case mentioned in Chapter 3. This might work, but then again it might not, and Gompertz probably wants to avoid the hassle and expense of a court case (see Chapter 18).

If Gompertz does want to control how the images are used, he should ask for copyright, preferably before the photographs are taken. This can either be included within a contract covering other matters, or it can be drawn up as a separate document, but in any case he also needs to think about the different ways in which the images might be used. There are separate copyright rights for different kinds of transmission, so you'd need to specifically claim all rights to do with 'communicating to the public', for example, which would cover the use of images on websites, rights to do with publication, etc. Standard licences do exist. It is also standard industry practice to charge reuse fees for subsequent uses of the same image, normally at a reduced rate, though in recent years some publishers have been squeezing photographers on this entitlement. So what does all that mean? If a magazine approaches Gompertz for an image of *Double Art History*, offering a fee, and Gompertz sells them one of the freelancer's images without getting the freelancer to license or assign copyright, can Gompertz keep the money from the magazine?

Well, on the one hand Gompertz is free to enter into contract with the magazine for absolutely anything he wants to agree to under contract law – all's fair in business. So, yes, in practice Gompertz could maybe get away with keeping the magazine's money. But there are a few issues to think about. For instance, is the magazine asking for exclusive 'all rights' conditions which would block Gompertz from selling elsewhere later? And is it asking him to supply images which are free from any copyright claims? The magazine would normally do so to protect the publishers from third-party liability – the bottom line here being that if the magazine found out Gompertz had supplied an image which had a disputed copyright or whose copyright he did not own, it might decide to use that as an excuse to rescind the contract, i.e. not pay him. Moreover, the magazine might be perfectly entitled to do so even if it had not asked for this copyright-cleared status, because it could be deemed to be part of the contract – as an implied term – that copyright in the images belongs to the person supplying them (see Chapter 5, the *Antiquesportfolio* case).

On a practical level it may come back to bite Gompertz later if Jack Bailey gets on top of his rights and his admin. So it is safer for a person in Gompertz's position to get all freelance photographers to sign something upfront.

This brings us to another question: can Bailey also approach the same magazine and sell the same image in competition with Gompertz? The answer is yes, unless Gompertz gets Bailey to assign exclusive publication rights to him. It's down to what is agreed between individuals and publications. For instance, a magazine like *Business Week* lets photographers retain copyright and syndication rights, as well as the right to payment for subsequent reuse, but claims rights to publish on the web, in foreign editions and joint ventures, and most of the proceeds from reprints (the commercial reuse for advertising purposes of editorial in the magazine). It's a tussle in which several people can simultaneously own different copyrights in the same work.

In practice, however, according to Euan Myles these niceties do not arise so often nowadays: 'If you don't give away copyright upfront these days you don't work; it's as simple as that.'

## People pictures: celebrities and non-celebrities

Great care needs to be taken with images of people following cases involving celebrities like Naomi Campbell. If you have shots of people – celebrities and 'punters' alike – separate privacy laws apply which could restrict your freedom to circulate the image, regardless of the copyright position. And if you are using a model, you may need to get him or her to sign a 'model release', giving consent for what you intend using the image and where it will appear (see Stern p.53, para 7.20).

## Don't forget moral rights too

Jack and Euan also have moral rights under copyright law (see Chapter 10) – so they could seek damages if they felt that there had been, for example, 'derogatory treatment', even if they had licensed the economic copyright to someone else. So, for example, if the magazine does not credit the photographer's name next to the image, or if the picture is used very inappropriately, in an odd context – perhaps on a piece of merchandising which the photographer considers to be sufficiently shoddy or lowbrow to cause him to fear that its existence for sale would undermine his reputation – the photographers could seek remedies (getting the item 'pulled', or damages, or both).

Lisa Lewis by Robin
Frowley, 2009.
info@robinfrowley.
co.uk

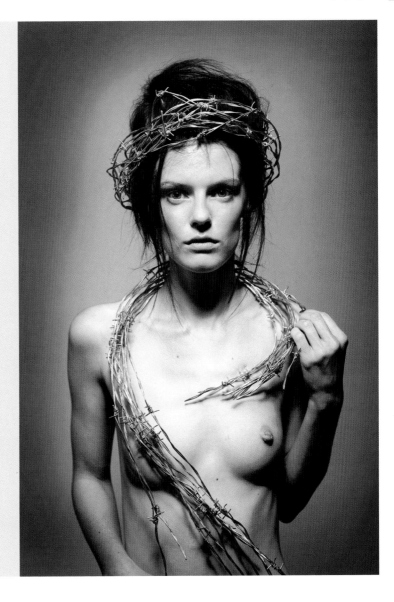

## Galleries and
## collectors beware

What I've said above about the photographer being the default
copyright owner can be important in relation to the commitments
of galleries or collectors to artists. Say a gallery has contracted with
an artist to control the exhibiting and publicity for an artwork they
have bought, and say the artist does not want to see any images of
his work unless you have cleared them with him first. Well, say the
gallery has the artwork photographed and they forget to ensure that

the photographer assigns copyright in the photo to the gallery. The upshot may be that the gallery loses control of how the image is used and that this upsets the artist.

## Museums and conservation

There are interesting points here for conservators and museums too. For instance, what if a photograph is restored? The restored photo could have a new copyright in its own right. Alternatively, the photographer or her trustees or successors could complain that a bad restoration was in breach of the photographer's moral rights.

## Summaries

### Photographs: Who owns copyright?

Is it a 'mechanical' or 'slavish' copy? (see Chapter 5, *Bridgeman* case.)

### Commissioned photographs

| YES | NO |
|---|---|
| The photograph may not benefit from copyright protection in the US but probably will in the UK. It is arguable. | Copyright attaches to the photo regardless of quality. Photographer owns copyright unless or until he licenses or assigns it away. |

Copyright always belongs to the photographer unless:

- there are any special circumstances which would make a court believe the commissioner had rights (applying trusts law: see Chapter 3, *Molino* case). This would be unusual and would not apply in Scotland.
- the photographer licenses or assigns copyright either in part or entirely to another or others (for the difference between licensing and assignation see Chapter 17).

**Note:** Even if photographers assign copyright they may still retain moral rights (see Chapter 10).

## Scenarios:

### What if two photographers take a picture of the same thing?

In a case involving an Oasis album cover, photographer A staged a set and took the picture, and another, B, came along and shot the

Euan Myles, *Camper in Glen Etivie*, 2004. Commissioned by The Scottish Government. info@euanmyles.co.uk

same thing without permission. B's photo went into *The Sun*. The court decided that whilst the unauthorised photograph was probably taken in breach of confidence, B's photo could not be seen as a copy of the official photograph, so copyright did not arise. Photographer A, the person who arranged the scene, did not own the copyright in the unauthorised photograph.

### What about photos taken without permission?

See the Oasis case described above, and also *Molino* (in Chapter 3), which looked at the question of the restaurateur's third party liability for allowing a freelance photographer to photograph the Princess Diana painting without the copyright owner's permission. The question was whether the restaurateur was liable for indirect copyright infringement for allowing this to happen. In that case the court said that he wasn't liable. He would have had to do something more than simply stand by and allow it to happen, such as a more positive act to facilitate or enable the picture. (Galleries and museums beware: this does no mean you are absolved from liability; you must always use public disclaimers informing visitors they are not permitted to photograph exhibits see Chapter 16).

**Get organised!**

Don't forget to claim DACS royalties on all published works and also public lending right royalties if you have been named as a contributor on any cover (see Chapter 17).

## INFORMATION BANK

www.euanmyles.co.uk

*Double Art History*: http://www.timesonline.co.uk/tol/comment/columnists/guest_contributors/article6805800.ece

www.robinfrowley.co.uk

Simon Stern, *The Illustrator's Guide to Law and Business Practice* (AOI, 2008).

For standard photography commissioning contracts see, for example, Wienand, Booy and

Fry, *A Guide to Copyright for Museums and Galleries* (London: Routledge, 2000), ISBN 0-415-21721-01.

*Oasis* case: *Creation Records Ltd* v *News Group Newspapers Ltd* [1997] EMLR 444.

For model release forms (adult and minor): see http://www.professionalphotographer.co.uk/Magazine/Downloads/Model-Release-Form

# 7

# Photography III:
# What can go wrong/digitisation

Digitisation has disempowered photographers to a large extent. Euan Myles (see Chapter 6) knows of friends who in the 1990s were making £50–100,000 every month from deals with picture libraries like Getty and Alamy – money enough to fund special trips to Africa, etc. to fund yet more pictures for yet more royalties. A self-perpetuating cash cow. But those heady days are gone. Stock libraries are using microstock now, and digitisation in general has weakened the ability of photographers to control and make demands about the use of their work. According to Myles, 'It's not great for your reputation as a photographer, either, if working to commission – to put images into stock. You are only going to annoy the clients who commission you direct – and they are the most important part of my business anyway. If I put images into stock now I more or less do it specifically for that purpose.'

Digitisation also enables diffusion of images that may not have been pre-planned. I know of many artists who are acutely aware of this: one who fell out with a gallery though the gallery still uses his images on its website; another who is fighting a museum because the museum, with her permission made digital copies of analogue images for a specific purpose (to enable them to make an audiovisual presentation for disabled people), but then was horrified to find that 15 of those images had been disseminated without her consent to the national press.

Common tactics for avoiding unlawful dissemination of digital pictures include making available only low-resolution images, using thumbnails only, or watermarking (see GettyImages.com for example).

Ten years ago there was a flurry of legislative activity both in the US and Europe, including the UK, whereby copyright laws were rewritten to make it a criminal offence for anyone to unravel copy-protection technologies (to decrypt something that has been encrypted, for example). The National Portrait Gallery/Wikipedia row centres on such an activity: the individual at the centre of the controversy had apparently 'unzoomified' images which the NPG had encrypted with Zoomify. Other protection technologies include Digimarc and ImageMagick.

But in practice this legislation is in fact, for once, in advance of real-world practice. Many artists and indeed image banks are still publishing completely unprotected images online: a small number of collections of images on the Visual Arts Data Service (VADS), for example, include watermarks, but the vast majority do not have them.

At the risk of scaremongering, if you are prepared to put unprotected images on the internet you should be prepared to see them copied somewhere. But if you have invested in protection technologies, copyright law can ensure that unlawful decryption is punished (leaving aside any separate arguments about things being in the public domain).

> **Tip:** I have been tempted sometimes to upload an image file onto a website to share it with someone: making it public in order to enable them to download it at the other end. If you want to avoid this you can email the file directly to them instead. YouSendIt.com is a free resource and allows upload and download of files up to 100 MB (or larger for a fee).

## INFORMATION BANK

Wikipedia: '"Microstock photography", also known as micropayment photography, is an offshoot of traditional stock photography. What defines a company as a microstock photography company is that they (1) source their images almost exclusively via the Internet, (2) do so from a wider range of photographers than the traditional stock agencies (including a willingness to accept images from "amateurs" and hobbyists), and (3) sell their images at a very low rate (anywhere from $0.20–10) for a royalty-free image.'

Wikipedia/NPG debate: http://www.eff.org/deeplinks/2009/07/eff-defends-wikipedia

VADS is the Visual Arts Data Service, providing an archiving service for arts digitisation projects in the UK higher and further education sector. It is based at the Library and Learning Services Department at the University for the Creative Arts. VADS provides online access to over 100,000 images that have been contributed by the education community itself, for free use in education. The collections cover a broad range of visual-arts subjects including applied arts, architecture, design, fine art and media, and have been contributed by organisations such as the Design Archives at the University of Brighton, the London College of Fashion, the Imperial War Museum and the Crafts Study Centre.

# 8

# Jewellery, Textiles, Garments, Sculpture, Furniture, Craft

> Dids Macdonald, CEO of ACID and former interior designer says she nearly lost her business several times through IP theft. 'You can never underestimate the importance of protecting your work,' she says.

## Fashion, garments, props and 'sculpture'

You might not regard a Star Wars white imperial stormtrooper helmet as sculpture, and the High Court didn't either (*Lucasfilm* v *Ainsworth*), but the fact that the courts even considered that it might be – and the fact that in an earlier case the judges did think the mould for a Breville sandwich toaster was sculpture – again shows the flexibility and oddness of the UK Copyright, Designs and Patents Act 1988.

The Star Wars case is important because it sets the current test for what the courts will currently treat as sculpture under the UK Copyright Act. The thing needs to be 'artistic', meaning that there needs to have been some 'artistic intent'. Contrast the situation with photographs (see Chapter 5: Photography I).

Other points from the Star Wars case are also worth noting:

- just because the thing has a function or use does not mean it cannot be sculpture
- even in the case of two identical things, one may be a sculpture and one may not be. If a thing has no artistic intent behind it, it is not a sculpture.

But this is upside down, is it not?

When you think about intellectual property law protection in general terms, copyright law, for me, should cover works of a slightly 'higher art', aesthetic nature whereas design protection should protect designs that are more industrial, perhaps functional – no less great for that, but different.

The older case, *Breville* v *Thorn EMI*, asserted that the sandwich toaster mould could be copyright-protected (flying in the face of a seminal case, *Hensher* v *Restawhile*, which discussed arts and crafts, 'artisan'-made artworks, specifically the prototype for a suite of furniture 'of distinctly lowbrow appeal' (Cornish & Llewellyn). And yet the Star Wars helmet was not copyright-protected.

Moreover, why does it matter if it is sculpture or not? The point of the case is that if the helmet had been seen as a sculpture under section 4 of the 1988 Act, it would have had the full force of copyright protection – for the lifetime of the creator + 70 years – including remedies available to the creator such as damages, destruction of any copyright-infringing item, and criminal sanctions. (By contrast there are at present no criminal sanctions for design right infringement, although ongoing lobbying activity before Parliament to change the laws in the UK began in 2009.)

However, this all seems a bit odd to me. Many of our greatest artists and architects have been involved in theatre stage set and costume design – Braque, Dalí, Matisse, Miró, Picasso, Pugin, Schinkel, Léger (see Chapter 10). You would have thought they had a better claim to copyright protection than the designer of a mould for a functional/industrial object. But the *Lucasfilm* case represents the current law.

## Fashion and garments

Fashion garments can attract copyright and/or design protection, but according to Nicola Solomon of Finers Stephens Innocent, 'EU community design rights are proving to be by far the most effective in securing designers' rights in the fashion sector.'

By registering an EU community design you gain a monopoly right to make, sell, distribute and license your designs, and a monopoly right to protect your work from infringement across the EU.

If you do try to use copyright to protect fashion designs, you need either to show that the garment is a 'work of art' or a work of 'artistic craftsmanship'. Strangely, the law of copyright with this kind of object has developed to the point where, for a 'work of art' in the works of 'artistic craftsmanship' category, you need to demonstrate a 'conscious purpose'. Again, this may not seem to make all that much sense in the real world, but behind this is the idea that one has to acknowledge 'higher art'/fine art on one level, and works like an Arts and Crafts table lamp on another. In a case involving a child's rain cape designed for mass production (*Merlet* v *Mothercare*) the court decided that there was no 'work of art' – the garment had been designed for purely practical reasons.

## Textiles

Sometimes the courts consider textiles to be copyright-protected because they are works of 'artistic craftsmanship'. But some textiles fail. Consider these three examples going in different directions:

- patchwork bedspreads and cushions not artistic or creative enough (*Vermaat* v *Boncrest*).
- the stitch structure of a fabric used in mass-produced designs created using a computer held to be a work of artistic craftsmanship (*Coogi Australia* v *Hysport*).
- hand-knitted woollen sweaters and cardigans designed and knitted by different people depicting among other things dancing lambs and golfing kiwis. The New Zealand judge decided these were entitled to protection as works of artistic craftsmanship (*Bonz Group* v *Cooke*).

See also the *Designers Guild* case in Chapter 4, where it was accepted that copyright subsisted in the Designers Guild fabric. There it was argued successfully that the second fabric had copied a substantial part of the first design, and that it had copied the first design substantially in qualitative terms, so as to be an infringing copy.

## Jewellery

Jewellery can be protected by both copyright and design rights. There is even a trade mark class for jewellery (see http://www.ipo. gov.uk/types/tm/t-os/t-find-class.htm: class 14). See Chapter 9 for a locket case study, and also the following cases:

### L. Woolley Jewellers Ltd v A&A Jewellery Ltd (No.1)

Design infringement. Woolley claimed that A&A had manufactured a pendant, for which two elements were almost identical to elements of a pendant designed by W. The two elements were: the bail (the little loop or attachment that connects to the pendant allowing the chain to pass through it in order to hang the pendant), the central portion of which was cut out in the shape of a heart; and a decorative edge consisting of a repeating heart motif. The claim succeeded in the first instance but was overturned on appeal. The judge was obliged to ignore the component parts of the design but

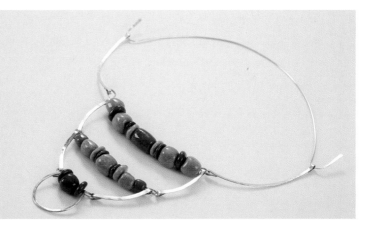

Kriket Broadhurst, three-tiered hand-beaten silver necklace with hand-crafted ceramic beads, 2005. kriketdesigns@gmail.com

needed to ask whether the design had been copied to produce an article substantially of the same design. This is different from the 'substantial part' test in copyright (see the *Designers Guild* case). For design rights here the court has to look at whether the whole design containing the copied element was substantially the same as the design enjoying design right protection.

This means an original design can be composed of parts that are not original; their combination in the final piece of jewellery is what matters (see Design Council in the Information Bank below).

### Blayney (t/a Aardvark Jewellery) v Clogau St Davids Gold Mines

This was a case about a gold ring and the value of its copyright. Blayney, a jeweller, sought damages from gold-mining company Clogau Gold, for copyright infringement. Clogau Gold engaged Blayney to manufacture a design (by Blayney) for a ring using their gold. After the business relationship ended, Clogau Gold continued to sell the ring using other manufacturers to make Blayney's design. Blayney argued in court that any of Clogau Gold's sales should be assumed to have been made by Blayney, unless Clogau Gold could prove otherwise. In other words, Blayney should get royalties on future sales. Clogau Gold said the value of the copyright was in the order of £250, so that was as much as Blayney could claim. An appeal court decided Blayney was entitled to damages calculated by reference to profits on lost sales and a notional royalty. Moreover, Clogau Gold's idea of a royalty of 2% was too low, so a rate of 5% was accepted.

This means that if your design is manufactured in future by someone else, you may still be entitled to royalties.

# INFORMATION BANK

**Star Wars case**: *Lucasfilm Ltd* v *Ainsworth* [2008] EWHC 1878 (Chancery Division). The helmets were not 'sculptures' under s.4 and therefore not protected by copyright. The ruling states: 'The stormtrooper helmet was not a sculpture. It was a mixture of costume and prop, but its primary function was utilitarian. It lacked artistic purpose'. The copying was not infringement because 'The clay stormtrooper head and the original clay armour were "models" within s.51 ...'. Regarding 'design documents and models', section 51 states: '(1) It is not an infringement of any copyright in a design document or model recording or embodying a design for **anything other than an artistic work** or a typeface to make an article to the design or to copy an article made to the design' [*emphasis added*]. Here, if the helmet is not a sculpture it is not an artistic work, so it was not infringing to make the 'article'. The decision of the Chancery court was affirmed on appeal in 2009 by the Court of Appeal: *Lucasfilm Ltd* v *Ainsworth*, 2009 WL 4666997, [2009] EWCA Civ 1328.

**Lobbying**: petition to the UK Prime Minister to Create a Law which Introduces Criminal Sanctions for Design Right Infringement: http://petitions.number10.gov.uk/DesignRight; and a Petition to Make Changes to the Copyright and Unregistered Design Right Infringement Damages Regime to Create Greater Deterrent against IP theft: http://petitions.number10.gov.uk/IPDamages.

The three bullet-point examples in the Textiles section of this chapter were taken from Simon Stokes's *Some Reflections on Art & Copyright*: http://www.oiprc.ox.ac.uk/EJWP0604.pdf.

*Vermaat* v *Boncrest* [2001] FSR 43: the copyright claim for secondary infringement (for the importation of infringing samples) failed on procedural grounds, but the bedspreads were in any case not considered to be works of artistic craftsmanship, being not artistic or creative enough.

*Coogi Australia* v *Hysport* [1998] 157 ALR 247.

*Bonz Group* v *Cooke* [1994] 3 NZLR 216.

Registering an EU community design: www.oami.eu.int

*Merlet* v *Mothercare* [1986] RPC 115

*Guild* v *Eskander* [2003] FSR 3. Claims that designs for wide, unstructured ethnic-style garments had been illicitly copied failed; the trial court held that the designs were not works of artistic craftsmanship and so could not be protected by copyright, but *were* 'original' and therefore deserving of protection under design right protection. The second part of the decision was reversed on appeal: the appeal court ruling that the predecessor designs were neither works of artistic craftsmanship nor 'original' so not protected by design right after all. This is a very interesting case for fashion designers, as well as for anyone interested in the legal implications of making 'mistakes' along the way to a finished work (here a mistake created in the making of a sample but perpetuated on purpose in finished designs) – a sort of serendipity most artists embrace as a positive rather than negative part of the process.

*L Woolley Jewellers Ltd* v *A&A Jewellery Ltd (No.1)* [2002] EWCA Civ 1119; [2003] FSR 15; (2002) 25(11) IPD 25078; *The Times*, 4th October 2002; (CA (Civ Div)).

*Blayney (t/a Aardvark Jewellery)* v *Clogau St Davids Gold Mines*, Chancery Division [2002] FSR 14; (2001) 24(10) IPD 24064; [2001] ECDR CN5.

Design Council: www.designcouncil.org.uk/en/About-Design/Business-Essentials/Intellectual-property/Ten-examples.

'Know your Rights to Jewelry Design', Sarah Feingold. www.beadandbutton.com/BNB/Objects/PDF/bbpdf070873.pdf. This article mentions beaders. It is broadly applicable to UK jewellery makers but be warned that it covers US law not UK law, so take care.

Cornish and Llewellyn, *Intellectual Property: Patents, Copyright, Trademarks and Allied Rights* (Thomson, Sweet & Maxwell, 6th edn, 2007).

# 9

# Design Rights and other IPRs

Copyright protects certain things and provides certain exclusive rights, but other kinds of applied art, craft, fashion or industrial design – as well as stationery and the general brand or get-up of your business – can be protected by other parts of intellectual property law, such as those concerned with passing off; with designs; database rights; with patents, trade marks and trade secrets; with confidentiality, unfair competition and, personality/privacy laws for photography (see Chapter 6).

Often these rights can overlap. For example, you could have both design right and copyright in the same thing; or you might be protected by the law relating to both trade marks and passing off.

## Passing off: 'moron in a hurry'!

Passing off is centred around a concept of 'deceptive resemblance'. Are you passing off your work as the work of another? (think 'Gucci' handbags, for example). Apparently, lawyers talk about passing off as the 'moron in a hurry test'! The *Designers Guild* case is important for explaining why copyright and passing off are different, as Lord Millett – one of the five Law Lords presiding over the case – explains: 'The gist of an action for passing off is deceptive resemblance. The defendant is charged with deceiving the public into taking his goods for the goods of the plaintiff. A visual comparison of the competing articles is often all that is required. If the overall impression is that "they just do not look sufficiently similar", then the action [for passing off] will fail.'

By contrast, the judge is saying, copyright is something altogether more complex. To decide whether there has been an unlawful breach of copyright you need to apply a technical test: the substantial copying test (see Chapter 4).

## Designs

Design rights, either registered or unregistered, apply to 3D shapes – such as jewellery, furniture, textiles, giftware and interior accessories (see Chapter 8). The right stems from section 213 of the Copyright, Designs and Patents Act 1988, for which see the Information Bank at the end of this chapter.

Computer graphics could also be protected by registered design rights. For instance, *Apple Computer Inc* v *Design Registry* decided that Apple Mac's onscreen icons, generated by the Apple Operating System, were protected by design rights.

You can choose to register your design, though you are not obliged to do so to obtain copyright protection in the UK (but see Chapter 18 and ACID's design databank service, for example). Deciding whether or not to register will depend on whether you can afford the £60 registration fee payable to the Intellectual Property Office, and also on the criteria in table 9.1, p.52.

If you are the creator of a design, you will be regarded as the owner of that design and thus entitled to apply for design registration unless:

- you have been commissioned for money or money's worth, in which case the commissioning person is the owner (Note how this differs from copyright: see Chapter 3).
- you created the design as an employee, in which case the employer is the owner.

You can search by proprietor, class, number or product to see if a product is already a registered design, by consulting the following webpage: http://www.ipo.gov.uk/types/design/d-os/d-find.htm. For EU Community designs see also Chapter 8.

## Case Study: the Bombo stool

In *Magis* v *Furniture Craft International*, ACID supported member designers Magis. Magis designer Stefano Giovannoni had created the Bombo stool, but an 'impostor' stool, the 'Tango', apparently identical apart from its low price, appeared on the market, undermining the whole business plan (according to ACID, from concept to market Magis had invested £500,000 in the Bombo).

ACID could have pursued the case under designs law, but decided instead to use the stronger protection of copyright law (on the basis that Bombo was a work of 'artistic craftsmanship'), to seek an injunction to stop sales of the Tango; to deliver up and destroy any Tangos; and to seek damages.

According to ACID CEO Dids Macdonald, 'Copyright is a longer-lasting right than other unregistered design rights and protects more features (for example, surface decoration would be excluded under

**Table 9.1:** UK Design Rights: Registered and not registered

| | UK-registered design | UK design right | Unregistered community design |
|---|---|---|---|
| **How do I get protection?** | You need to register your design with us | Automatic right, no registration required | Automatic right, no registration required |
| **How long does protection last?** | 25 years from the filing date of your application | 15 years from the end of the calendar year where the design was first recorded in a design document or, if a design is made available for sale or hire within five years, ten years from the end of the calendar year that first occurred | Three years from the date the design is first made available to the public |
| **Type of protection** | Monopoly protection | Exclusive right against copying. A licence of right is available for the last five years of protection | Monopoly protection |
| **Can I renew this type of protection?** | Yes, you must renew every five years up to the maximum period of 25 years | No | No |
| **What does it protect?** | The overall appearance of the design, excluding features dictated by function | Only three-dimensional aspects of your design, excluding surface ornamentation | The overall appearance of the design, excluding features dictated by technical function |
| **Originality** | Your design must be new, so not identical to an existing design, and have individual character | Your design must be original, so not copied from an existing design, and not commonplace | Your design must be new, so not identical to an existing design, and have individual character |
| **How much does it cost?** | £60 to apply for a single design | Nothing | Nothing |
| **How easy is it to enforce?** | No need to prove that your design was directly copied to enforce your rights | You must prove that your design was directly copied to enforce your rights. You must also keep a record that proves the date your design was created | No need to prove your design was directly copied to enforce your rights |
| **Can I sell it?** | Yes | Yes | Yes |
| **Does it give me protection abroad?** | You can extend your UK protection to certain countries, mostly members of the Commonwealth. Further information is available from www.ipo.gov.uk | Reciprocal protection is only available in a limited number of territories. Further information is available from www.ipo.gov.uk | Protection is only for countries within the EU |

Bombo Stool, designed by Stefano Giovannoni, year of production 1997. Image reproduced with kind permission of Magis. www.magisdesign.com

UK unregistered design right), and there are certain exclusions which are not part of copyright law but which apply to industrial designs. In the absence of a registration, copyright is a more effective right than other unregistered rights and can be enforced in other jurisdictions more easily.'

Currently there are no criminal sanctions available for design infringement, but there are moves afoot to get this changed (see Information Bank).

According to Dids Macdonald, 'Since ACID's formation in 1996 we have seen a huge escalation of copying taking place within the design industry. Before that I nearly lost my design business several times over due to intellectual property theft. We have to be aware of our rights and be prepared to take robust action when needed.'

## Copyright and design right simultaneously?

### Case study: locket by Gillian Davies and Polarity

Polarity has registered a US copyright for lockets which she makes from recycled steel car parts, soldering on an eyehook through which she threads a simple ball chain. A button badge-type lid is held in place by a strong magnet. The lids are decorated with all sorts of designs from different artists. It is a funky industrial design; not very 'high end' but arguably unique in its own way. It is sold to a younger, trend-conscious market.

We both sell the same locket through the online shop Etsy: Gillian Davies on Carousel Monkey, Polarity on Polarity (see Information Bank). I use my own photographs of the lockets on the online shop. Polarity makes her own arrangement for photography so separate copyright exists in relation to her photographs.

I have sold the real property rights in the actual artwork (here a handmade artist's-proof one-off screenprint, entitled *Carousel*), but I still retain copyright in the photographic image (subject to what I said about photographer Paul Ditch, see Chapter 5).

Trying to analyse the locket as an example under UK, rather than US, law, I spoke to Andrew Lee of McDaniel & Co. Lee confirmed that since I had no input into the design of the locket itself but only the artwork which was applied to it, I was not the 'designer' for the purposes of assessing whether a design right arose in the locket. However, if I *were* the designer – or the locket itself had been dealt with under technical legal provisions called the 'first marketing' provisions under the design right legislation – then Lee's instinct was that the locket is not a copyright work in the sense of not an artistic work such as a sculpture or work of 'artistic craftsmanship' – unlike, say, a handcrafted piece of furniture, which could potentially have both copyright and design protection depending on how it was made and the intention of the maker (see Chapter 8). However, Lee was not in any doubt that my artwork itself is of the type that would attract copyright protection, and as the creator I would be the first owner of any copyrights.

In terms of UK design rights, we might think that the locket in itself could be protected for its shape and configuration. However, Lee felt that as the shape of the locket seemed relatively standard and similar to lockets that have been around for many years, the locket itself might fail to get an unregistered design right, because it might be considered to be 'commonplace' in its shape and configuration. The artwork which is applied to the locket has copyright in itself, but as an element of the locket design it would be excluded in terms of

This locket is an artists' collaboration between Gillian Davies and US maker Polarity. artwork © Gillian Davies (lawandarts@ aol.com); locket design US © Polarity (Uncorkeducation@aol.com). Photography Paul Ditch. fixed.focus@ymail.com

unregistered design rights as 'surface design', and therefore would not form part of any design right protection (see table 9.1). 'What could arise in the combination of the shape of the locket and the artwork', says Lee, 'is EU unregistered design right, which protects both the shape and surface patterns of a product for a period of three years usually from the first sale in the EU. This situation is different from the *Woolley Jewellers* case (see Chapter 8) in relation to the UK unregistered design right because that case involved the combination of two commonplace 3D elements being put together as a new design which was capable of being protected by UK design right. Here, one of the elements that has been combined is the 2D surface pattern (the artwork), which is excluded from UK design right protection and hence could not be taken into account to assess whether a new UK design right arises – leaving only the potential problem that the shape of the locket on its own is commonplace.'

This is a particularly difficult and untried area.

A registered UK design would cover 'the overall appearance of the design, excluding features dictated by function', which seems to suggest the functional design aspects provided by Polarity are excluded, but perhaps my artwork dictating the 'overall appearance' could achieve the status of registered design? I'd need to apply and pay to find out. You must renew a registered design every five years.

Apart from anything else, the locket example shows how more than one person can have intellectual property rights – and copyright – in the same thing. And that is even before you start licensing.

## Trade marks

If you get involved in merchandising or creating an identity though logos, etc., you may come across trade marks. These are symbols (like logos and brand names) that distinguish goods and services in the marketplace. So, for instance, Levi jeans are protected by trade marks, as are the logos of brands like M&S.

You need to register a trade mark and the rules are quite stringent. To obtain a registered trade mark there must be a sign capable of being represented graphically (including textually) by which the goods of A can be distinguished from those of B.

If you have a registered trade mark then you are permitted to use the ® sign to indicate that the mark is registered. It is an offence to use the ® sign if the mark is not registered. Using the ™ sign simply means that you are using the particular sign in a trade mark sense – i.e. to brand your goods – but that the mark itself is not registered.

You can trade mark colours in the sense that a particular colour is used in a particular way to be suggestive of your design/corporate image and no one else's, but you must specify the colour(s) you want to protect by a colour code (such as a Pantone reference), and you need to refer to a 'specific arrangement of colours habitually used'. (See the *Libertal* case in the Information Bank).

Some 3D shapes can be trade-marked too, but again the shape has to be very specific: recently the EU courts refused trade marks to multi-coloured dishwasher and washing-machine tablets and the 1951 rounded-ends and chevrons of the chocolate Bounty bar, because the shape did not 'depart significantly from the norms and customs of the sector to enable the average customer to distinguish immediately and with certainty the product concerned from those of other undertakings'.

Trade marks have been used differently in different cultures: for example, some folk art has been trade-marked in Tonga, Panama, Fiji and New Zealand, to prevent rival sales of 'fakelore'. In the UK this kind of issue could also be dealt with by the law on passing off.

You must renew a trade mark every ten years. For more on whether to think about registering a trade mark, go to: http://acid.eu.com/ip-doctor-faq

## Patents

Patents are more for inventions (e.g. the Dyson vacuum cleaner) and are unlikely to apply to most artworks.

# INFORMATION BANK

Design rights: Table from http://www.ipo.gov.uk/ types/design/d-applying/d-before/d-needreg.htm

Bounty bar: European Court of First Instance, Luxembourg, 8 July 2009, as reported by Telegraph.co.uk

*Apple Computer Inc.* v *Design Registry* [2002] FSR 38, reinterpreting the Registered Designs Act 1949 ss.1(1), 1(3), 44(1) to take account of upcoming changes in the law as required by EU Council Directive 98/71.

Etsy/CarouselMonkey: www.etsy.com/shop. php?user_id=6983138

Etsy/Polarity: http://www.etsy.com/view_listing. php?listing_id=25415126

Folk art: Māori arts board of Creative New Zealand: www.toiiho.com

EU trade marks: www.oami.europa.eu

ACID http://acid.eu.com. Andrew Lee of McDaniel & Co. has a regular column called IP Doctor available on the ACID website.

ACID's petitions to change design law and damages for IP infringements: http://petitions. number10.gov.uk/DesignRight/http://petitions. number10.gov.uk/IPDamages/

Footnote: In the locket collaboration example, Polarity's locket has a US copyright. This is quite different from UK copyright. In the States a designer like Polarity with an article like this must clear the US 'separability' test hurdle, which states that 'the design of a useful article ... shall be considered a [copyrightable] work if, and only to the extent that, such design incorporates pictorial, graphic or sculptural features that can be identified separately from, and are being capable of existing independently of, the utilitarian aspects of the article'.

*Libertal* case: Out-law (Masons) summary: http:// www.out-law.com/page-369

# 10

# Artists' Moral Rights

Moral rights belong to the artist. They are supposed to be less about property (intellectual property or real property) and more to do with the *personality* of the artist.

It is often thought that whereas copyright rights – the economic rights – can be assigned or licensed, moral rights are perpetual and inalienable. Actually, whilst moral rights cannot be assigned to another person (because they are personal to the artist [s.94]), they can be bequeathed by Will and artists can waive moral rights (1988 Act, s.87) in writing, and indeed are often asked to do so in contracts.

Moral rights derive from the French system. There are a lot of US cases, but UK law is different so care needs to be taken with the examples below.

There are various moral rights in world legal systems deriving from the French cases, but the following are enshrined by the UK Copyright, Designs and Patents Act 1988:

1   the right to be identified as author or director
2   the right to object to derogatory treatment of work
3   the right to privacy of certain photographs and films (this overlaps with other privacy rights which attach to photographs of people: see Chapter 6).

## 1. The right to be identified as author or director

For the UK, the right to be identified as author or director, see 1988 Act, s.77. In other legal systems this is known as the right of paternity.

Guille, a painter, agreed to deliver to a dealer, Colmant, his entire future production for a period of ten years, at a rate of at least 20 paintings per month. The contract said that the works sent to the dealer should be signed with a pseudonym and the painter would not sign any earlier works still in his possession. A dispute arose and Colmant sued Guille for breach of contract. The French Court of Appeal said that Colmant could not prevent Guille from using his real name in connection with works he had created, in spite of the contract.

Note that the Guille case involves a dealer asking the artist to refrain from adding his name to his work, which was found, in France, to be unlawful. This right also applies to the right not to have words falsely attributed to you if you never said them (e.g. *Moore* v *News of the World*, where the newspaper published an article headed 'How My Love For The Saint Went Sour', attributed to a singer 'talking to [a reporter]', concerning her married life with her former husband, a James Bond actor. The court found that despite the report's interview format, it nevertheless had falsely attributed the words at issue in that case.

Stern cites the example of a cartoonist who had assigned the copyright in his cartoon. The original was a black and white line drawing but an advertising agency used it, colourised, while keeping the cartoonist's signature on their colourised version. The cartoonist successfully sued in court for 'false attribution'. The agency would have been better off using the image without his signature, but was probably trying to do the right thing. Better still, they should have cleared it with the artist.

In another current case I know of, an artist is suing a national magazine publisher for publishing an article which the artist believes was passed off as research and written content done by the newspaper writer, whereas the artist believes it is her content; she is also not happy that the reporter spoke to curators rather than to her; she accuses the publisher of misrepresenting, 'misogynising' and 'sensationalising' her original content, and of publishing an article which is 'full of historical inaccuracies'. Another of the artist's complaints is that, whilst the article purported to be a review of the art show, the exhibition title was excluded, as was the artist's name.

For the right to be identified as author or director to kick in, the artist must have signed the work (be 'identified on the original or copy, or on a frame, mount or other thing to which it is attached') or must 'assert' that right (s.78), in words like these: *'The right of Gillian Davies to be identified as the author of this work has been asserted in accordance with ss.77 and 78 Copyright, Designs and Patents Act 1988.'* That assertion is binding even if it is no longer visible (see 'Museums' in Information Bank).

This author/director provision does not apply to computer programs, to typeface designs, to computer-generated works, or to works produced by employees; and it will not apply in cases of 'incidental inclusion' nor if fair dealing/current affairs news reporting applies, nor if you have agreed to include your work in a magazine or book (see 1988 Act, s.79). It also does not apply to works where the creator died before 1st August 1989.

## 2. Derogatory treatment (also known as the right of integrity)

The right to object to derogatory treatment of work (see 1988 Act, s.80) can apply, for example, to the cropping of photos; to merchandising or overprinting images with text; to placing images in inappropriate contexts; and to stretching or distorting of graphics.

Section 80 throws up some odd situations. It has already been suggested that an art collector could completely and utterly destroy a work purchased from an artist, but cannot in any way film or publicise that act of destruction, and cannot exhibit a mutilated or cut-down or partial version of the original work.

So the following was *not* derogatory treatment: Clementine Churchill's burning of Graham Sutherland's portrait of her late

Euan Myles, *Dog No.1*, personal work; 2001. The artist specifically requests that we 'do not crop', and he is entitled to do so. info@euanmyles.co.uk

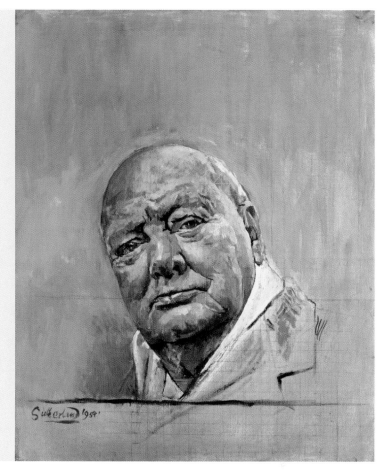

First sketch for the portrait of Winston Churchill (1874–1965), by Graham Sutherland (1903–80), oil on canvas, 1954. Private Collection/The Bridgeman Art Library. In copyright until 2051.

husband Sir Winston Churchill, presented to him by Parliament, which the widow justified on the grounds that he had always hated it because it made him look 'half-witted'.

This is similar to the French right of integrity, which is nicely illustrated by the following Buffet example.

### Bernard Buffet: *The Refrigerator/Still Life with Fruits*

A court allowed Bernard Buffet to put a stop to an auction sale of a painting on metal billed as *Still Life with Fruits*. The work had been separated from another piece, *The Refrigerator*, in which Buffet had decorated a fridge with three painted panels on the front, one on top and two either side, originally intended to be auctioned in Paris for charity. He had signed only one panel. Nine fridges had been similarly decorated by other artists and exhibited in a gallery. Buffet was entitled to prevent the sale of separate pieces of the original work.

### 1980s Italian films cases

Filmmakers Federico Fellini and Pietro Germi sued commercial TV stations for interrupting the artistry of their films $8\frac{1}{2}$ (*Otto e mezzo*) (1963) and *Serafino* (1969) with too many commercial breaks, invoking human rights protection as enshrined within the Italian Constitution. Fellini failed but Germi succeeded, though he would not have done if they had given their approval (contractually presumably, with the TV channels) to the 'mutilations'.

There is no need to 'assert' the derogatory treatment right.

### Fernand Léger

Léger was commissioned to design sets for the opera *Bolivar* by Darius Milhaud. He completed the commission. The opera was performed in 1950. In 1952 it was re-performed with the omission of two scenes. Léger objected and sued on moral rights grounds. The court agreed he had copyright and moral rights but found that the composer and producer also had rights, including the right to control the production. It ordered that Léger's permission ought to have been sought before any cuts were made, and decreed that an explanatory note about the omission should be publicised in all advertising for future performances.

### Illustrators: Cropping and overprinting

Stern points out that when the 1988 Act was going through Parliament, the advertising lobby was very vociferous, affecting a change to the draft so that only treatment which is unusual and not reasonably to be expected is infringing. So, according to Stern's view, overprinting and cropping may well not fall foul of the artist's right of integrity (Stern para 7.25). For overprinting see also the *Molino* case mentioned in Chapter 3 (the case also touched on the example of a matchbook which had overprinted artwork).

Other interesting moral rights (not UK)

- the right of divulgation – the right to withhold work and to decide whether, when and how it is displayed
- the right of modification and the right to 'repent or retake' if the artist pays an indemnity

- the right of inheritors/trustees after the artist's death to attribute works as being those of the deceased.

### James McNeill Whistler: *Brown and Gold, Portrait of Lady E*

Whistler painted Lady Eden for her husband in 1893, agreeing that the fee would be 'between 100 and 150 guineas'. He exhibited the completed painting under the title *Brown and Gold, Portrait of Lady E*, and in the meantime Lord Eden sent the artist a cheque for 100 guineas. The artist was insulted (but cashed the cheque). When the painting was returned to his studio, Whistler painted out Lady Eden's head and painted in another, refusing to deliver the painting to Lord Eden. Lord Eden sued for restoration and delivery of the portrait plus damages. The courts agreed that he should have his 100 guineas back, but would not force the restoration or delivery of the portrait.

## Remedies

If you find you have a case for moral rights there are various kinds of legal injunction you can obtain. For example, if you are an architect it could be possible to order a developer to name you on a building. Or you could get an injunction to have a broadcast or publication 'pulled' if it allegedly involves 'derogatory treatment'. Or a publisher may have to print a disclaimer or statement disassociating or distancing you, the artist, from the work as published. Damages could also be awarded, possibly with an 'aggravated' or 'exemplary' element – but the sums involved would probably not be as large as those sometimes seen in defamation cases.

## INFORMATION BANK

All of the examples cited in this chapter, except the 1980s film scenario, are from Sir John Henry Merryman, *Law, Ethics and the Visual Arts*, Wolters Kluwer Law & Business, 5th edn, 2006 (ISBN-13: 9789041125170). Merryman also cites a lot of fascinating (US) examples, relating to the destruction or partial destruction or modification of public art, sculpture and murals.

1980s filmmakers: Christoph Beat Graber and Gunther Teubner, 'Art and Money and Constitutional Rights in the Private Sphere' in *Oxford Journal of Legal Studies* 18:1, pp.61–73.

Museums: Wienand, Booy and Fry, *A Guide to Copyright for Museums and Galleries* (Routledge 2000), p.69. ISBN 0-415-21721-01.

*Moore* v *News of the World* [1972] 1 QB 441; [1972] 2 WLR 419.

Simon Stern, *The Illustrator's Guide to Law and Business Practice* (AOI, 2008). Cartoonist: para 7.29.

# 11

# Defences I: Matisse case study

As already mentioned, you can quite happily bumble along and not upset anyone copyright-wise, or not be upset copyright-wise. If you are working privately and not overtly reaping economic rewards from the efforts of others, no one will necessarily know or care, or have cause for a copyright action. (That is not to say that if you are using things privately you are not under any obligation to clear copyright – it depends what you are doing – but it is in many ways a practical matter.)

One sure-fire way of causing major upset is to publish an image without permission – in copyright law this is the sticky area of 'issuing works to the public'. The point about publishing is that it is a high-profile activity. Other activities may be just as unlawful under copyright rules, but publishing is overtly public; and with publishing come clear economic benefits, to publishers, authors and all the copyright owners involved – we should recall that copyright was in fact 'invented' to prevent others from unlawfully benefiting from the sweat of another's creative labour. 'Publication' is one of the most obvious exclusive rights which copyright accords the copyright owner (ss.16, 18 and 19, 1988 Act).

An important case here is *Matisse* v *Phaidon*, where the estate of Henri Matisse was unhappy because in 1992 Phaidon Press Ltd published Matisse images, allegedly without permission, in its glossy coffee-table publications *The 20th Century Art Book*, *The Art Book* and *Minimum*. The case did not go to court but was settled (see Information Bank).

Although each picture was correctly labelled and attributed, the Matisse family wanted an injunction to stop the publisher using Matisse pictures in its books, an order for 'delivery up' and destruction of books already including his images, and damages. The settlement included an injunction preventing the publisher from publishing more books in future without a licence; and payment of royalties + interest for past publications.

Henri Matisse (1869–1954), *Dance (I)*, Paris, March 1909. Oil on canvas, 259.7 x 390.1 cm (8 ft 6½ in. x 12 ft x 9½ in.). © Succession H. Matisse/DACS, London 2010. Digital Image: © 2009 MoMA, New York/ Scala, Florence. www.scalarchives.com

Phaidon Press did not deny that it used the images, but offered two alternate defences:

1  that its use of the images was for the purpose of criticism and/or review, and therefore a permitted use under the Copyright Act's 'fair dealing' defences (s.30(1))
2  and/or it had a license already – an historical one, dating from 1977, granted to Phaidon's predecessor company by Matisse's French copyright agents.

On the first point the Matisse family basically said there was not criticism or review because the book was mainly a picture book and the little text that accompanied the images was merely descriptive rather than 'critical'. For example, the following passage set beside an image of the saturated colours of the Fauvist painting *The Dance* in the *20th Century Art Book* they thought fairly 'lightweight':

> Set against a blue and green background, five pink figures dance joyously in a circle. They twist and turn their bodies with feeling as they lose themselves in the rhythm of the dance ... The vivid colour scheme and the expressive freedom of the women are characteristic of the bold palette and uncompromising hedonism of the Fauves, of whom Matisse was the leading exponent ... His fascination with Near Eastern art ... Along with Picasso, Matisse is widely held to be the greatest genius of the twentieth century ...'

This issue was not argued in court, which is a shame as it would have made an interesting case. There was a lawyers' case management conference, however, during which it was evidently agreed that whether or not this was an example of fair use and criticism/review could be decided by a judge, and not by (art) experts (although in the event the issues did not go in front of a judge). Phaidon paid a sum in the settlement, implying the publisher agreed that the Matisse side had a good case.

This is a bit like recent skirmishes relating to parodies of Damien Hirst's work. There is a bit of a power imbalance with 'big name' artists who can afford to wield their copyright powers, but the law should apply to all.

In practice publishing a Matisse image is extremely vexatious: we need consent from the Matisse Estate, from DACS and also from the image owner; and the Estate will want to see proofs. The requirements of rights clearance run counter to the linear schedule of every normal publishing production department so using a 'big name' picture is always difficult (the Matisse Estate needed to see page proofs of this chapter inclusive of text and picture: but the publisher did not get to that stage until the very end of the production process, as is standard industry practice, so to make changes at the Estate's behest at that stage would be very expensive, time-consuming – even impossible).

This particular artist author would like to think that this situation would encourage publishers to buy from lesser known artists instead of wading through a DACS-type rights system, but sadly there is no evidence of this! But it does have to be recognised on a pragmatic business level that editors and picture researchers might on occasion steer clear of the 'powerful' copyright owners in favour of getting things published on time – and that the complications of getting copyright clearance these days are such that it is little wonder people pinch images and hope for the best (see Chapter 15).

## INFORMATION BANK

Source: An article by the Matisse family's lawyers, Suzanne Garben and Ruth Hoy, entitled 'Coffee Table Art Books – Unfair Dealing?', in *Entertainment Law Review*, 19 (2000), supported by DACS, who manage UK copyright in Matisse's work.

*The Dance*: the image reproduced here may be an earlier version of *The Dance* than that reproduced by Phaidon Press as discussed above.

# 12

# Other Defences

You might hear that it is OK to do something because it is 'fair use'. This is actually US law; UK law's defence to copyright infringement refers to 'fair dealing'. The main things this covers are:

- s.29   research and private study
- s.30   criticism, review and news reporting (see the Matisse case study in Chapter 11)
- s.31   incidental inclusion of copyright material
- s.31A  making a single accessible copy for personal use
- s.31B  making multiple copies for visually impaired persons.

On a sliding scale you can 'get away with' more on copyright if you are an 'educational establishment', less as a private individual, and even less if you are doing business (the latter being able to rely on few defences).

## Parody

UK law does not actually specifically say that parody is a defence: if parodying a work, you need to rely on s.30, i.e. to be able to say that it is 'criticism or review' (or that you have not copied the work or a substantial part of the work) – or make a claim for 'false attribution (s.84); or use the law of passing off. An interesting case here involved Glenn Brown's 2000 Turner Prize entry *The Loves of Shepherds 2000*, which either copied or was inspired by Anthony Roberts's science fiction book jacket for the Robert A. Heinlein novel *Double Star*, published in 1974. The case was settled out of court. At the time of writing, images of both works were still available via Google.

## Differences in UK and US law

Incidental inclusion, a UK defence, provides an interesting illustration of the fact that UK and US copyright law can differ quite dramatically.

Incidental inclusion would apply where, say, a film crew shoots a street scene and a bus drives by bearing some advertising photography. The film studio would not need to clear copyright with the photographer or advertiser, being able to say that the photograph was 'incidentally included'.

But in the US a medical artist tried to make a copyright claim where his illustrations appeared in the background of a TV advert for text messaging: enlarged versions of two of his works appeared without permission, one of which was visible in the advert for 10.6 seconds, and another for 7.3 seconds.

The medical artist lost his case but it went as far as a US Court of Appeals, whereas in the UK he may not have got that far as the advertiser would probably have been able to avail itself of the UK copyright defence of incidental inclusion.

## INFORMATION BANK

Copyright, Designs and Patents Act 1988

s.31 Incidental inclusion of copyright material.
(1) Copyright in a work is not infringed by its incidental inclusion in an artistic work, sound recording, film or broadcast.
(2) Nor is the copyright infringed by the issue to the public of copies, or the playing, showing or communication to the public of anything whose making was, by virtue of subsection (1), not an infringement of the copyright.

Thank you to Masons/Out-law.com for their report on the medical illustrator (dated 25/11/2003).

# 13

# Architecture

Architecture can be protected by copyright under the following designations:

- the building as an 'artistic work'
- architectural drawings as 'graphic works'
- models as artistic works.

Building features can be protected either as copyright works or as designs.

In a rare Scottish copyright court decision of Lord Bannatyne (Outer House, Court of Session) in *Donal Toner* v *Kean Construction (Scotland) Limited and CRGP Architects and Surveyors*, Toner alleged infringement of copyright by Kean and CRGP in respect of architectural plans which he prepared for a development in East Kilbride. Kean and Toner parted company and Kean appointed CRGP as its new, successor architects. Toner has argued that he has not been fully paid for his work and that, therefore, there is no implied licence granted to Kean and to CRGP to use his architectural plans. Toner alleged that CRGP had directly infringed his copyright by using a substantial part of the plans to obtain an amendment to a planning consent; and also that Kean had indirectly infringed his copyright by constructing a building in conformity with those plans. The case began in 2005. Kean and CRGP failed to defeat a preliminary case on procedural grounds in 2009 and so the case could proceed to full trial probably later in 2010. It will be an interesting test case for copyright and architecture if it does go to trial, but according to Toner's advocate, the case may be settled out of court in the meantime.

Someone in Kean's situation should obtain a licence, probably expressly, but legally a license could also be *implied*, say, where an architect has been engaged to take a design to the stage of drawings suitable for construction and has been paid for their efforts.

Building reconstructions are not captured by these limitations; works to reconstruct a building do not infringe copyright in the building or in any drawings or plans which were followed.

**2D→2D; 2D→3D;
3D→2D**

## 2D→2D

One architect's drawing copied in a drawing by another could lead to infringement of copyright (2D→2D). So in the *Toner* case, Toner alleged breach of copyright insofar as CRGP had copied substantial parts of Toner's architectural drawings, which were then used in support of Kean's planning application.

## 2D→3D

A house constructed in accordance with an architect's plans can be a copy of those plans. As with all other types of copying, it is not necessary for the original to be replicated in every respect. What matters is whether the copy is of the work as a whole or any substantial part of it (see Chapter 4). So in the *Toner* case, the alleged breach of copyright in relation to Kean was that they had constructed the buildings following the drawings prepared by CRGP, which in turn had copied Toner's drawings (indirect copying).

## 3D→2D

There is no copying, however, where a graphic work, photograph, film or broadcast is made of a building, though photographers may wish to use a property release form (see Information Bank).

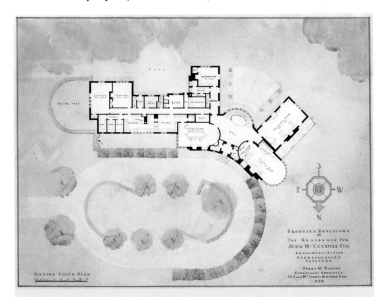

Perry Duncan (architect), ground-floor plan of Gribloch House with proposed revisions, 1938. © courtesy of RCAHMS. Licensor: www.rcahms.gov.uk

## Design rights

There are a few court decisions involving design elements within architecture. The *Ultraframe* case (2002) involved designs for a 'Quickfit' conservatory roof construction system. The case is of interest only in that it confirms the 'copyright belongs to the employer not the individual' point: there the court decided that the designer's drawings were made on the company's time and using its equipment, suggesting an 'employee' relationship, so the design right belonged to the company and not to the individual.

In *Scholes Windows Ltd* v *Magnet Ltd*, which came before the English Court of Appeal in 2001, the issue was whether or not an unregistered design was 'commonplace', so as to determine whether UK design right protection applied. The design in question was an integral feature of a top-opening casement window going by the name of Nostalgia. The feature was a decoratively shaped horn extension of the kind used at the end of the stile on the upper light of timber-frame Victorian sash windows. The ruling examines section 213 of the Copyright, Designs and Patents Act 1988.

The question was whether the design lost its originality, and thus its copyright protection, because it was a commonplace design. The Court of Appeal agreed with the trial court that it was necessary to compare it with other designs from the 'design field in question at the time of creation' (i.e. to look at other designs that existed and could conceivably have been copied at the time) when deciding that issue. Both trial and appeal courts agreed that there had been no design right infringement as the design in question was indeed commonplace.

## Moral rights

Architects have the right to be named wherever photographs of their buildings are published or if the buildings are filmed, but also on the actual building (or buildings if the same design is constructed more than once; 1988 Act, s.77; see Chapter 10).

# INFORMATION BANK

Section 4 of the Copyright, Designs and Patents Act 1988 defines an 'artistic work' as including: '(a) a graphic work, photograph, sculpture or collage, irrespective of artistic quality' and '(b) a work of architecture being a building or a model for a building', among other things, and also states that '"building" includes any fixed structure, and a part of a building or fixed structure'.

Section 17(3) states:
"In relation to an artistic work copying includes the making of a copy in three dimensions of a two-dimensional work and the making of a copy in two dimensions of a three-dimensional work."

*Toner* v *Kean and CRPG* [2009] CSOH 105: the preliminary case is at http://www.scotcourts.gov.uk/opinions/2009csoh105.html (17 July 2009). Search on www.scotcourts.gov.uk for the trial hearing (Court of Session), which may or may not happen.

*Ultraframe* case [2002]: http://www.designcouncil.org.uk/en/About-Design/Business-Essentials/Intellectual-property/Ten-examples/

Property release forms: http://www.professionalphotographer.co.uk/Magazine/Downloads/Model-Release-Form

s.17 Infringement of copyright by copying:
'(3) In relation to an artistic work, copying includes the making of a copy in three dimensions of a two-dimensional work and the making of a copy in two dimensions of a three-dimensional work.'

# 14

# Is an Image Out of Copyright?

**Case Study:
Bridgeman Art
Library**

The Bridgeman Art Library is a fanatstic and beautiful resource for art images. In 2009 Bridgeman published a list of artists going 'out of copyright' that year, including Ernst Ludwig Kirchner, Vittorio Guaccimanni and Charles Doudelet. In 2010 artists coming 'out of copyright' (i.e. the 70th anniversary of the artist's death, counting from the end of the calendar year in which the artist died) include illustrator Arthur Rackham, Gwen John and Alphonse Marie Mucha.

However, be warned: just because an artist is out of copyright does not mean an image will be free to reproduce, as licensing fees may still apply. Bridgeman (and other art libraries) normally needs

Arthur Rackham (1867–1939), illustration from *Alice's Adventures in Wonderland* by Lewis Carroll (1832–98), 1907. Private Collection. Photo: Christie's Images/The Bridgeman Art Library (image reference CH19609). Nationality/copyright status: English. Came out of copyright in 2010.

Alphonse Marie Mucha (1860–1939), 10 crown banknote of the Republic of Czechoslovakia, 1920. 8.6 x 11.4 cm (3½ x 4 ½ in.). © Mucha Trust/The Bridgeman Art Library (image MCA178468). Nationality/copyright status: Czech. Came out of copyright in 2010.

to charge a fee to cover both copyright and reproduction rights. Copyright may be cleared via Bridgeman, or there may be further hurdles to clear. For example, to use the Winston Churchill image (p.61) I had to clear it with the Estate of Graham Sutherland, who in the event very kindly granted copyright permission for no fee. But I did have to pay Bridgeman a reproduction fee – that is, a fee to reproduce the photograph of the artwork – as Bridgeman owns the rights in the photograph. Such reproduction fees are scaled according to whether you are printing the image across a full page, half page or quarter page. Copyright no longer has to be cleared to enable the use of works by artists who are out of copyright, and therefore there is no copyright clearance fee. But the reproduction fee probably still applies, so with the image of a Czech banknote by Art Deco artist Mucha, above, even though only reproduction fees applied, not copyright, in fact the cost of reproducing it was only reduced by one-third compared with what it would have cost if the artist had still been in copyright.

## INFORMATION BANK

www.bridgemanart.com

# 15

# Trying to Do the Right Thing

Even in putting together this book, I stumbled across vast problems in trying to secure copyright clearance on images. What if you do not keep the source details? Or you see a picture but do not know the name of the publication or the photographer? Or you don't know anything about the image at all? Is there any way of doing a visual trace online so that we can give the proper credits and get copyright clearance?

There are tracking services out there, but they seem to be pitched at the level of big commercial image banks with thousands of images to clear. And the basic advice given by DACS is that it is 'best not to publish if you cannot trace the copyright owner'.

Alternatively, the high- or higher-risk tactic is to treat the image as an 'orphan' work, and use it with a form of words like these: 'Every attempt has been made to identify the copyright owner for this work and to obtain permission to publish it. If you wish to contact us regarding this matter please do so by contacting ...'. However, that could be a risky business so either you or your company or lawyer needs to make a careful judgement.

The idea with 'orphans' is that you must carry out 'due diligence' and make every effort to find the copyright owner. In this book I have tried to pass on the identity of the copyright owner under each plate by providing an email address or website address. This seems like the sort of pragmatic approach it would be sensible to adopt in future.

## The future for 'orphan works'

The UK government spent time in 2009–10 considering legislation to enable licensing bodies to deal with 'orphan works' – copyright works whose authors can't be found (see p.79). The background to the Digital Economy Bill 2009–10 is to be found in the report *Digital Britain 2009*, which said that:

> the expectation is that anybody wishing to use orphan works will be
> expected to secure an appropriate permission from the Government first,

and permission will only be granted where the proposed operator can satisfy the Government that the business methods and procedures involved satisfy key minimum requirements, including making appropriate searches for the true owners and making provision for the reimbursement of rights holders who are subsequently found and claim for the use of their work.

This is a major issue. The British Library estimates that 40 per cent of its archive counts as orphan works. Mass digitisation projects, which could put forgotten works digitally back onto the cultural map, are thwarted because of the orphan-works problem. Anyone who uses orphan works on a commercial scale currently risks not only civil but also criminal liability.

Photographers are concerned that photographs posted online regularly lack identifying metadata, and hence evidence of ownership is lost. Orphan works are being created in growing numbers.

Not only do creators lose a source of income, but important cultural assets remain unobtainable because of the legal difficulties associated with using these works.

The *Digital Britain* report proposed a two-pronged 'promise':

- 'I promise I made appropriate searches for the true owners'; and
- 'I promise to make provision for the reimbursement of rights holders if subsequently found'.

However, this has not yet been passed into law. The advice must currently still be 'tread with care', or even 'do not use', if you do not know the copyright owner. Proposals for a new centralised body to help individuals and organisations get copyright clearance on images where the copyright owner cannot be found have for the moment been jettisoned.

## Other problems

Of course, sometimes the problem is not that you don't know who owns copyright but that either they refuse to answer your request or they charge too much. Or there are multiple copyright owners you need to ask, which is administratively and financially burdensome. Or the publisher who you think owns the copyright in a particular work upon closer inspection turns out not to, because it did not get the correct permission itself when the work was published.

In this book, for example, in order to illustrate Chapter 11, I wanted to use a Matisse image. But that involved getting permissions

77

from DACS as the collecting society for the Matisse Estate; and from the Matisse Estate, who wanted to see a colour pdf mock-up of the pages as they would appear in the finished book (which is not really possible according to publishing-industry practice, as by the time the pages have reached that finished state it is impossible for a publisher then to pull out a plate or pages of text). Moreover, even after I had cleared those two hurdles, neither DACS not the Estate actually had the image to give me. I had to research where the painting actually resides – which turned out to be New York's Museum of Modern Art – then ask MoMa for the image, which was then passed on to the Scala image agency.

The alternative for me in that case – or in the *Designers Guild* case outlined in Chapter 4 – would be to 'publish and be damned', i.e. to use the image anyway, without permission, but rely on one of the copyright defences, namely, either that

- this is 'fair dealing' because it is criticism and review (see Chapter 11)
- or this is the reporting of a legal case under the copyright exception in CDPA 1988 s.45(2) (though that looks very unlikely to work here, as that section of the Act is really for publishers like Butterworths [LexisNexis], Sweet & Maxwell or Merrill Corporation, who take raw court transcripts and turn them into law reports).

The basic principle remains the same: you should be asking the artist/originator for permission, and thus giving them the opportunity to set any limits on the use of the artwork and/or charging a fee (see also the cartoonist example in Chapter 10).

## INFORMATION BANK

Orphan works: The treatment of orphan art is governed by an international law, the Berne Convention, which broadly states that if a copyright work is anonymous or pseudonymous, or the author cannot be found by reasonable enquiry, it is reasonable to assume that the author died more than 70 years earlier, and so any copying of the work is permitted by law. (Source: Own-it/Gowers report: http://www.artquest.org.uk/artlaw/copyright-now/orphan-works.htm). Proposals to alter UK law in 2009–10 were abandoned in April 2010 when the Digital Economy Act 2010 passed into law minus a controversial clause 43 (of the Bill of the same name) that had been drawn up to help those seeking to licence 'orphan' works by establishing a new system of intermediary agencies who would have supposedly helped find the copyright owners of images (along US lines). Clause 43 of the Bill was axed due to lack of Parliamentary time to adequately scrutinise the details, all time having been used up by the seemingly more pressing issue of ISP liability for illegal file sharing. Artists, and photographers especially perhaps, may be relieved that UK law remains unaltered, since some feared that such a system, badly implemented, could have hindered and not helped individual artists' rights: that the changes would have operated like a Trojan Horse, opening the floodgates to widescale legitimised theft of all works of art – especially photography; especially on the internet. (See the Association of Illustrators' position on photography: www.theaoi.com, 'Notes re. s.42 [sic: actually it was clause 43] Digital Economy Bill' [members only]). For what could have happened in the UK, and for the current situation in the US, listen to an interesting radio interview with Brad Holland for the Illustrator's Partnership, in which Holland gives a lucid and detailed account of US artists' concerns, available online (Google search for Mark Simon interview with Brad Holland on April 5, 2008). 'Clause 43' may be asleep and not dead, however, as it may be revived in another form in the UK in the future.

Copyright, Designs and Patents Act 1988, s.45:
's.45 Parliamentary and judicial proceedings.
(1) Copyright is not infringed by anything done for the purposes of parliamentary or judicial proceedings.
(2) Copyright is not infringed by anything done for the purposes of reporting such proceedings; but this shall not be construed as authorising the copying of a work which is itself a published report of the proceedings.'

# 16

# Who Cares Anyway?

With the internet comes a lack of regulation, and as a result little pools of self-regulation. Copyright falls readily into the self-regulatory field. Movements like Copyleft and Creative Commons have sprung up to allow creators to manage their own intellectual property and to make public (and therefore open to 'reuse'/'theft'/copying) those bits of their work that they feel happy to share. So, for example, if I look up 'Banksy' on http://search.creativecommons.org – I get images which are free for me to use.

These private/community developments stand in sharp contrast to laws like the American Digital Millennium Copyright Act 1998, which has as a central tenet the outlawing of any technology or any person found to be 'unlocking' or decrypting any other technology that has been used to try to protect copyright. It would outlaw, for example, any software that unscrambled a watermarking program – think about Zoomify, the software used by the National Portrait Gallery to protect images in its database by breaking the images up into little tiles like a mosaic; and 'unzoomify', the program used allegedly by Derek Coetzee to put the pictures back together again (see Chapter 9). There are similar EU (and UK) provisions.

Banksy (as in 'Copyright is for losers!') has recently been seen to bypass the normal rules surrounding copyright – this time in the field of gallery exhibitions and the usual prohibition on the public against taking photographs of artworks.* He has taken a uniquely practical approach, by displaying a handwritten postcard with the following message: 'If you take photos please buy a badge [*double strike through with the words 'sold out'*], postcard, sticker or t-shirt.'

The artist, usually described as 'anonymous graffiti artist', is more or less saying, 'If you take a photograph you are taking a bit of my intellectual property. I trust you not to exploit this economically but please do acknowledge my rights by spending a little money on my merchandising so at least I get something out of it' – or something along those lines, accepting that to stop people taking photos altogether is unrealistic.

........................

* Galleries could be found guilty of 'authorising' copyright infringement if any members of the public were to photograph works of art and then reproduce them commercially (see further, Keith Wotherspoon, 'Copyright Issues Facing Galleries and Museums' in European Intellectual Propery Review (EIPR) 25(1), 2003, 34–39).

80

To put it another way, according to Yasmin Joomraty of Laurence Kaye Solicitors, this is Banksy 'successfully connecting with the exhibition-goers in exploiting his copyright. He understood his target audience and made them understand the give-and-take of his creative endeavour.'

Banksy's online shop and the copyright notice there is similarly straightforward: 'Everything in the shop is free, simply download the file and process the artwork. Please note: this shop is for personal amusement only. Please don't use it to start a business. Thanks.'

For Joomraty, 'This keeps the artist in control and highlights the fact that the works do have a value arising from rights which only the artist is entitled to exploit (even if he chooses to exploit these rights by allowing free downloads).'

There are also social web tools like Flickr, Facebook and Twitter. I personally put my art, and my blog, on Facebook and on b-uncut.net, despite knowing it is not 'safe' – that Facebook or anyone else could easily take the images. But because I have not reached any level of fame or importance as an artist and because in fact I have sold a few paintings as a result of making them public in this way, I prefer to call it 'marketing'. However, one person's marketing is another's stupidity, so whether you take this route or not is a personal choice.

## INFORMATION BANK

Yasmin Joomraty 05/08/2009: 'Laurence Kaye on Digital Copyright' blog at http://laurencekaye.typepad.com/laurence_kayes_blog

Banksy shop: http://www.banksy.co.uk/shop/index.html

About Creative Commons: http://creativecommons.org/videos/wanna-work-together

Gillian Davies's blog: http://carouselmonkey.blogspot.com

# 17

# How Much Money Can I Get?

The potential value of copyright in artworks has been unequivocally demonstrated in a recent development involving photographer Annie Leibovitz, whose financial difficulties have been attentively followed by the international press. According to an article in Art Monthly (April 09), Leibovitz was able to raise US$24 million (c.£15m>) in loans from Art Capital Group by 'mortgaging' her photographic negatives, real estate, contract rights and existing and future copyrights (presumably on the basis of looking at her expected lifespan and adding on 70 years' worth of potential) as collateral. Such an undertaking is not unusual in the field of literary copyright, but is quite significant in the world of visual art.

At the time of writing, news stories are breaking of alleged breaches of the contract (failure to make repayments) by the 59-year old Leibovitz, followed by renegotiations that entail allowing the photographer to delay repayments and/or buy back copyrights. It seems it may not be as easy as it looks to give away absolutely all control over your work. One of Leibovitz's most famous images – a 1980 print showing a nude John Lennon in a foetal position over Yoko Ono – sold at Phillips de Pury & Co. in London in 2007 for £18,000.

'Normal' (non-celebrity) artists should make themselves aware of less controversial routes to earning some money out of copyright.

## Artist's resale rights

For reasonably well-established artists who can sell work at €1000+ (c.£880), you should contact DACS or ACS (see Chapter 19) to apply for artist's resale rights royalties.

| Resale price (€) | Royalty % amount due |
|---|---|
| From 1,000 to 50,000 | 4.00% |
| From 50,000.01 to 200,000 | 3.00% |
| From 200,000.01 to 350,000 | 1.00% |
| From 350,000.01 to 500,000 | 0.50% |
| Over 500,000 | 0.25% |

## DACS Payback

If you are a painter, sculptor, printmaker, illustrator, photographer, cartoonist, animator or designer, and your work has been used in television programmes broadcast on BBC1 or BBC2, ITV or Channel 4, or has been reproduced in books, magazines or journals, you may have a valid claim for a share of a pot of money collected by DACS on your behalf (the fund is usually around £300,000 each year but many artists fail to claim what is theirs). This could be a significant amount. For instance, in 2009, the highest payment to an individual was £5450, while the average payment to an individual was £250. The minimum payment is always set at £25 for successful claims.

Each year, by 30th September, you can claim for all works published or printed up until December of that year, and this includes retrospective claims for past years. So if you suddenly remember something that was published nine years ago, just claim now – go as far back as you like. It does not matter for DACS Payback purposes if you are named in the publication – unlike the public lending right (see below). And it makes no difference whether inclusion of the image is incidental. So if you painted an illustration that's on a bus that is clearly seen in a BBC drama, you should claim. Likewise it does not matter if the image is on a cover page or inside a publication: these are all treated the same for the purposes of Payback.

## Public lending right for named contributors

Another place to go is www.plr.uk.com. Public lending right was set up by the Government in 1979, giving authors and illustrators the right to a small payment each time a book is borrowed from a public library. For 2007, it was 5.98p per lend. You don't need to own the copyright – but you must be credited as illustrator/contributor on the title page. '[In 2007] We paid out £6.66 million to 23,942 writers, illustrators, photographers, editors and translators in our annual payments in February,' says James Parker at the PLR. The 'average payment was £278.' To qualify for PLR in a book you should be named on its title page or be entitled to a royalty payment from the publisher – but you do not have to own the copyright. In terms of annual deadlines, say for this book publishing in September 2010, I would need to register the book by 30 June 2011 in order to be credited PLR payments on library loans recorded since 1 July 2010.

**Reuse fees**

It is normal to expect to sell an image for publication for a fee, and then to be paid a smaller sum for 'reuse' of the same image by the same publisher in subsequent publications. This, again, is being squeezed, but it has been standard for a long time so there is no reason why you cannot negotiate this.

**Royalties or rights?**

Be aware that you can get both royalties and rights payments, say, if you are an illustrator publishing a book.

Royalties are a share of the publisher's profits from manufacturing the book, calculated as a percentage of the retail price of the book. You might get 5–15% of the cover price of the book, for example, depending on your deal with the publisher.

Rights payments are lump sums for rights to certain things: for example, if the publisher wants to create merchandising, you could get a merchandising rights deal worth around 50–80% of profits.

Such payments are unfortunately all subject to your own negotiating skills. If you do not have such skills – and most artists don't – get advice.

**Assignation or licence?**

Remember that if you assign copyright the person getting the assignment will own the work entirely and can use it in whichever way they choose in perpetuity. You might not even be able to use your own work even for something like your own website unless you think of that and make sure you say you need that use. So ask for more money if you are assigning rights.

If you license work you can keep some or all copyright rights, but be aware of the following issues:

- Which territories are covered – UK, Europe, worldwide?
- Is it an exclusive licence? An exclusive licence can act like an assignation and block your own use of your work.
- How long does the licence last – six months, one year, five years, perpetuity?
- What about usages/rights? (print, digital; e.g. are you keeping or giving away rights to publish a paperback edition of a hardback work; or are you keeping or giving away rights to enable merchandising to be made using your image?)
- What about print runs and web traffic? (e.g. have you asked to be paid a further feee should a publisher want to reprint a successful

book? or if an online page featuring your work attracts a lot of attention online?)

- Is it a front cover, double-page spread, full page or incidental piece?

Essentially, the more you allow the other side, the greater the fee you should negotiate for yourself to offset the loss of those potential future incomes.

Simon Stern provides a very useful list of the different usages and royalty rights at para 10.78 of his book for illustrators. But the list applies more widely than to illustrators – and could be taken to apply to all visual art creators.

## INFORMATION BANK

Leibovitz: Henry Lydiate (of ArtQuest), "Leibovitz Futures" in *Art Monthly*, April 09, p.325.

Simon Stern, *The Illustrator's Guide to Law and Business Practice* (AOI, 2008) pp.102–3.

For reuse fees see the National Union of Journalists, www.nuj.org.uk

# 18

# Getting Legal Advice

There are two big problems here: 1) trying to reverse mistakes or avoid problems; and 2) working out what to do – and associated fears about employing lawyers.

Dealing with part (1) is quick and easy, because basically you cannot correct mistakes. If you assign copyright or grant any kind of exclusive licence, there is no clawback, 'except in some very limited, highly technical situations,' says solicitor Nicola Solomon, consultant in the IP/Media Department of Finers Stephens Innocent.

> 'The general rule is that you cannot go back. The message is to take yourself and your art seriously and seek legal advice before signing things. No one inviting you to contract is your friend ... so do not be naïve about it'. (Nicola Solomon)

On (2), the following comment by an artist attending an Own-It training event on copyright law in Newcastle is typical: 'The problem with having lawyers doing training presentations is that they assume you're potentially going to employ them. In many cases, the cost of employing one of them for recovery may be more than any award or compensation you may get. And if your work has been stolen by a big company, they'll have the financial backing to defeat any small claim every time.'

There are a few things to say here by way of comforting artists afraid of big lawyers' bills. Going to court is gigantically expensive: you could pay a sum running into five or six figures. You can try to hire your lawyer on a 'no win, no fee' basis, but you may have a very high insurance premium to go with that. However:

1 issues are often resolved without going to court; a single lawyer's letter may be all that is needed
2 mediation can be a useful alternative to litigation (but a CEDR

[see http://www.cedr.com] could cost around £4,000, so you need to have a high-value claim to make this worthwhile)

3 the small-claims procedure does not involve lawyers; so if you lose, the worst-case scenario is you pay the court fee (10% of the amount you are claiming for in the dispute), plus costs associated with witnesses and out-of-pocket expenses.

Another artist seeking legal advice in London reported to me that DACS was 'not very good', referring her toward a £250 per hour solicitor, and also failing to direct her to a broadcasting union which in the event was useful ('albeit that they didn't really seem to understand copyright law in relation to installations'). The artist was fortunate enough to stumble across a free solicitor at Toynbee Hall in London – they run a sort of citizen's advice service – who started getting things moving for her.

## Other free sources of help

There are not many organisations to whom you can turn for free advice, but there are the following:

- Trade associations and unions. You will probably need to become a member to access legal support. Unfortunately, the National Artists' Association in London, the artists' union, is now defunct.
- Own-it offer a free initial advice message via their website, and run training events.
- ACID has tried to address evidential problems associated with the UK's no-registration requirement by creating a databank, which, according to CEO and former interior designer Dids Macdonald, now contains some 300,000 images, 'demonstrating the need for such a service'. ('The government Office of Harmonization for the Internal Market (OHIM) database recording registered designs also holds around 300,000 images – but that represents 27 countries. We have that for the UK alone,' says Macdonald). ACID is very strong on design rights.
- The Gowers Report did recommend that such a voluntary register be formalised in the UK, to be set up by the end of 2008 by UKIPO. This has not yet happened.
- Briffa also offer 'DesignProtect' insurance, which may also be worth considering. But look around for other insurance deals (e.g., on the UK Insurance Index (see Information Bank), look for art insurance).

- In Scotland there is the Innovator's Counselling and Advisory Service for Scotland (ICASS). There is also the Intellectual Assets Centre's www.ia-centre.org.uk

To find an art lawyer you can also contact the Law Society, in either England & Wales or in Scotland.

Sadly artists still feel powerless in the copyright arena. I am watching with interest a new battle between an Etsy illustrator and a large stationery retailer being played out on Twitter. Sometimes the 'name and shame' route seems more effective to individuals.

## E-commerce and the internet

Despite the dangers of digitisation discussed above, and the loss of control, etc., e-commerce can be your friend. The legal landscape has been technically changed because regulators realised from around 1999 that consumers and sellers could suffer unfairnesses if things were being sold 'at a distance', i.e. via websites. Protections for customers were beefed up in Europe and the US to make sure that consumers have strong rights to return goods and receive refunds when buying online; and rights given to online sellers, like artists with copyrights, were strengthened by a mechanism known as 'third party liability'.

What this means in essence is that, taking the example of a craftsperson/maker selling on Etsy.com, if she has reason to believe another seller is selling copycat products, she should contact Etsy and file a notice of copyright infringement with the website (each site will have different policies and terms and conditions, so be aware of those). It is likely that the shop will prevent the seller from selling further products, because the host seller, Etsy, do not want to be 'third-party liable' for the actions of its individual sellers. The same would be true for other online shops and image banks.

So a practical solution normally prevails without detailed arguments being entered into on the merits of whether or not something is actually in breach of copyright. If you do want to argue the merits, see above for enlisting the help of a lawyer.

# INFORMATION BANK

For information on exceptional and complex circumstances in which an assignment of copyright can be implied, see Simon Stern, *The Illustrator's Guide to Law and Business Practice* (AOI, 2008), Appendix D, p.127.

Finers Stephens Innocent LLP: www.fsilaw.com; FSI represents the Association of Illustrators.

Small claims: www.moneyclaim.gov.uk

CEDR: www.cedr.co.uk

ACID: www.acid.uk.com; membership fee (unless turnover is £50,000+) £172.50 inc. VAT – 20% off for affiliated trade associations, e.g. DACS.

Briffa www.briffa.com/design.php

www.own-it.org

www.icass.co.uk

UK Insurance Index www.uk-insurance-index.co.uk/art-insurance-1.html

Simon Stern, *The Illustrator's Guide to Law and Business Practice* (AOI, 2008).

# 19

# Can Artists be Prevented from Repeating their Own Work?

Gillian Davies,
*Mandolin Angel*
(detail), May 2009.
Collage/mixed media,
overall 70cm x 70cm
(27½ x 27½ in.).
© Gillian Davies,
lawandarts@aol.
com/Paul Ditch Fixed
Focus Photography
fixed.focus@ymail.
com

> 'Those who do not want to imitate anything, produce nothing.'
> *Salvador Dalí*

Artists have always repeated their own work, and nowadays galleries encourage, even pressurise, artists into repeating successful images. But the situation with copyright is awkward and confusing (just for a change).

Gillian Davies, *Yellow Angel* (detail), September 2009. Collage/mixed media, overall 80cm x 118cm (31½ x 46½ in.). © Gillian Davies, lawandarts@aol.com/ Paul Ditch Fixed Focus Photography fixed. focus@ymail.com

Look at the glorious court tapestries commissioned by Henry VIII in the 16th century. Series like the *Triumph of Petrarch* tapestries are beautiful, rare and valuable commodities indeed: in monetary terms they were worth a similar sum of money to a fully rigged battleship of the day. So it is no surprise then that the artist/maker and his workshop repeated the same design from original cartoons for different clients. There is direct evidence of at least two or three copies made from the cartoons of the *Triumphs* of *Time* and *Eternity*, made for Cardinal Wolsey in the early 1520s; of another set made for Louis XII; and possibly yet another for Wolsey in 1525 (albeit possibly modified with different border designs or – given a more extreme 'twist' – with two figures inserted, including the Cardinal himself).

However, the 1988 Act does purport to restrict such repeating if copyright has been assigned:

> s.64. Making of subsequent works by same artist
> 'Where the author of an artistic work is not the copyright owner, he does not infringe the copyright by copying the work in making another artistic work, provided he does not repeat or imitate the main design of the earlier work.'

What this appears to mean is that if you assign copyright, say, to a person who has commissioned a sculpture for her garden, or a mural for his staircase, you can repeat that sculpture or mural for someone else only if it does not 'repeat or imitate the main design'. This as usual is a question of degrees and context and subjectivity, and some case law here would be useful. But at the moment there is none.

I am not sure how often this might apply in practice, as most artists do not ever 'repeat' work, in the sense that each creation will usually be individual because it is hand-crafted, as it were. I, for one, probably couldn't repeat a painting even if I tried. But it could well apply, for example, to textiles/apparel designers (who commonly churn out hundreds of designs per month), or to a printmaker, who has assigned copyright to a supplier. This might well be taken as another reason never to assign copyright: but in practice it is down to how strong you feel in the negotiations: balanced against your desire to keep working and keep being paid.

You should also bear in mind that if you promise not to repeat the work at all – if you sign a contract with some form of words saying you will never do the same work again – you may well end up binding yourself more strictly than section 64 does. All's fair in business, so be careful what you agree to.

In short, if you have assigned copyright, in theory you need to be very careful about repeating work; if you have not assigned copyright, repeat away, if you can.

## INFORMATION BANK

*Triumph of Petrarch* tapestries: *The Burlington Magazine*, September 2004, vol. CXLVI, No. 1218.

# Resources

## Books

All artists, not just illustrators, should look at Simon Stern, *The Illustrator's Guide to Law and Business Practice* (Association of Illustrators, 2008). Written by an illustrator, it is a very practical, very useful book, with sections on contracts and licences, fees and agents. The latest edition has a new section on royalty agreements.

Also useful to all (and not just to museums) is *A Guide to Copyright for Museums and Galleries* by Wienand, Booy and Fry (Routledge, 2000). ISBN 0 415 21721 01. (http://www.museumscopyright.org.uk/guide.htm)

*Digital Copyright: Law and Practice* by Simon Stokes (Hart Publishing, 3rd edn, 2009) is a useful update on UK law, and is good on software/computer copyrights. ISBN 9781841139326

## Websites

**ACID**: offers advice to members, has a free copyright advice column on its website, runs a voluntary scheme for registering designs with its databank, and offers members 'copyright protected' stickers and tape for use with CDs, etc. Membership costs from £172.50 per annum. www.acid.uk.com

**ACS**: the Artists' Collecting Society (ACS) was formally established as a collecting society in June 2006 to collect resale royalties (*droit de suite*) on behalf of artists in the UK (see Chapter 17). ACS was set up in response to requests from artists and from their dealers, via the British Art Market Federation (BAMF) and the Society of London Art Dealers (SLAD), for artists to be provided with a choice of collecting society for the management of the artist's resale right. If an artist has not mandated any particular society then the collecting society which manages both copyright, in general, for all artists and the artist's resale right will be deemed to be mandated. Currently DACS is the only society which meets this criterion. Therefore any artist who has not mandated another society will be deemed to have mandated DACS to collect on their behalf. www.artistscollectingsociety.org.uk; http://www.ipo.gov.uk/pro-types/pro-copy/c-policy/c-policy-artist/c-policy-artist-guidance.htm

**AOI**: the Association of Illustrators will provide illustrator members with free advice on copyright. Membership costs £75 (students), £132 (associated members/not yet commissioned) or £156 (full members). www.theaoi.com

BCC: the British Copyright Council is an umbrella organisation for members like DACS and AOI and does not provide advice, but it does have some useful Information Sheets.
http://www.britishcopyright.org/

BIPP: the British Institute of Professional Photography provides legal advice to members and has a useful page on copyright for photographers. Membership costs between £50 and £150.
www.bipp.com/copyright.html

CLA: the Copyright Licensing Agency provides some basic copyright information.
www.cla.co.uk/copyright_information_aboutcopyright.php

DACS: 'the UK's leading copyright and collecting society for artists and visual creators'. It provides three rights-management services for artists: payback, the artist's resale right, and copyright licensing (see also Chapter 17). www.dacs.org.uk

IAL: the Institute of Art & Law runs seminars and distance-learning courses (certificates and a diploma) in art law for lawyers and arts professionals. They have a series of publications that includes detailed summaries of art copyright cases.
www.ial.uk.com

IPO: the Government's Intellectual Property Office has good basic advice on copyright and designs law, and you can search on registered designs. Look out also for updates on a consultation on moral rights which closed in September 2009.
http://www.ipo.gov.uk

CGA: the Copywatch Giftware Association provides members with a free 'design watch deposit' scheme, limited free advice and discounted legal advice. Membership costs between £100 and £846 depending on turnover.
http://www.ga-uk.org/copywatch.htm

Contracts: Giles Dixon's ContractStore offers a standard design agreement for £45 + VAT for designers working to commission (either retaining copyright or not), an art gallery/artist agreement, and a multimedia contract. http://www.contractstore.com/design-agreement

Fashion: UK Fashion Exports helps members with business issues including copyright. http://www.5portlandplace.org.uk/index.php

IA-Centre: Glasgow-based Intellectual Assets Centre may help Scottish artists.
http://www.ia-centre.org.uk

ICASS: the Innovator's Counselling and Advisory Service for Scotland.
http://www.icass.co.uk

NUJ: the National Union of Journalists publishes a useful *Freelance photographers' guide to digital costs.*
www.nuj.org.uk/innerPagenuj.html?ac=1&docid=157

Own-It: an intellectual property advice service for creative businesses providing a free email advice session, they also run free copyright training courses. www.own-it.org

# Index